The
Skirtmaking
Book

The Skirtmaking Book

Patricia Riley

B T Batsford Ltd London

To my husband Neil
and also to Fiona, Neil, Chris
and John

© Patricia Riley 1979
First published 1979

ISBN 0 7134 1641 6

Filmset in 'Monophoto' Sabon by
Servis Filmsetting Limited, Manchester

Printed in Great Britain by
The Anchor Press Ltd, Tiptree, Essex
for the publishers B T Batsford Limited
4 Fitzhardinge street, London W1H 0AH

Contents

Introduction

During this century there has been a skirt revolution. Throughout most of our history skirts have been long until during the 1920s when dresses and evening gowns had skirts above knee length. Since then skirts have been one of the major topics of the fashion world. The line, the length, the fabric, have all ranged over an unbelievably wide spectrum of change. Today, for many people, the skirt is one of the most important items in their wardrobe, worn in a variety of styles for a wide range of activities.

A skirt is a good starting point for a beginner dressmaker. The processes involved may be few and simple. Basically, they are machining and neatening seams, putting in a zip, attaching a waistband and turning up a hem. The final result can be a useful and attractive garment, often lower priced than its ready-made counterpart.

Particularly where personal body measurements do not compare with standard measurements, skirts and tops are practical and comfortable to wear. Here too, making a well-fitting basic skirt pattern is time well spent. This makes it so much easier to make a skirt, avoiding the considerable effort involved in fitting during construction since this can be difficult, it not impossible, where no help is available. Many beginners, after their first success with the basic pattern make this classic style again and again in a wide variety of fabrics.

The urge to develop and experiment with more advanced styles and processes often follows. Flares, frills, pleats, decorative detail give individuality to a skirt, making it appropriate for every occasion from the everyday skirt for work to sportswear or something suitable for the most formal occasion.

This book describes skirtmaking from the simplest level to the most advanced, covering every aspect from design to choosing fabrics and carrying out the necessary processes in the best way according to the effect wanted and the fabric being used.

Making a simple skirt to personal measurements

A flattering skirt, which is well-made and comfortable to wear is an invaluable asset to a wardrobe. However, with the standardisation of sizing which is a major feature of the ready-to-wear clothing market, many people who are not stock sizes are unable to get a skirt to fit them.

For a skirt to fit well, three measurements must usually be taken into account; the waist, the hip and the length. For the waist measurement, the tape measure must be fitted closely round the natural waistline. The hip measurement is taken round the widest part, in the region of 20 cm below the natural waistline. The skirt length is measured down the centre front, from the waist to the required length, which is influenced, of course, by personal taste and fashion.

Using these measurements a foundation pattern or block can be drawn.

To make a simple pattern the basic equipment consists of:

2 sheets of paper approx 100 cm square
Tape measure
Pencil and rubber
Straight edge, preferably a metre stick
Scissors

For more advanced pattern making it will be useful to have a few more items of equipment:

French curve   Set square
Quarter scale square Pattern notchers

Equipment for pattern making

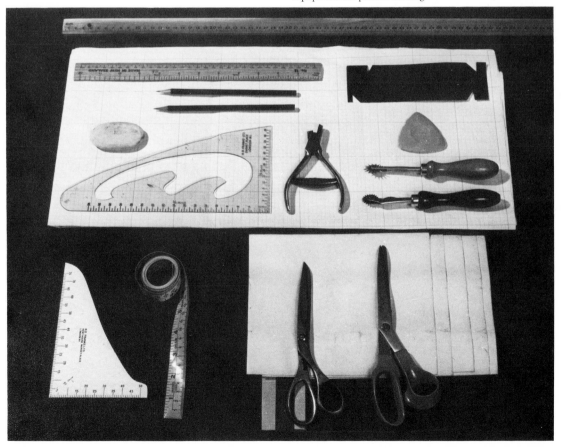

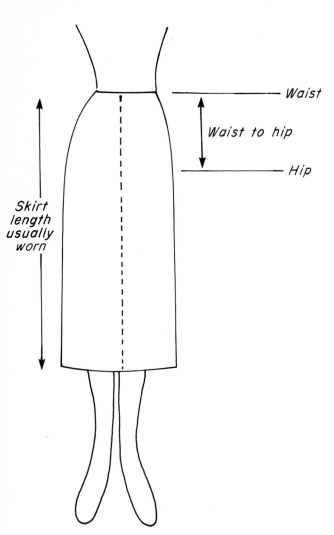

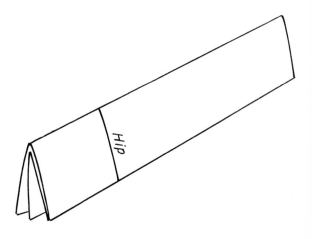

Flared foundation pattern

To make a very simple foundation pattern for a skirt without darts which fits smoothly at the hip and has some flare, the first step is to take the waist, hip and length measurements, wearing the usual foundation garments and a smooth underskirt.

1 Draw a rectangle. The measurements should be half the waist plus 5 cm × length.

2 Draw in the hip line 20 cm below the waistline.

3 Cut the rectangle out.

4 Fold the rectangle into four lengthways and cut along the folds, making four strips.

5 Lay the strips on the second piece of paper. Keep them just touching at the waist and spread them

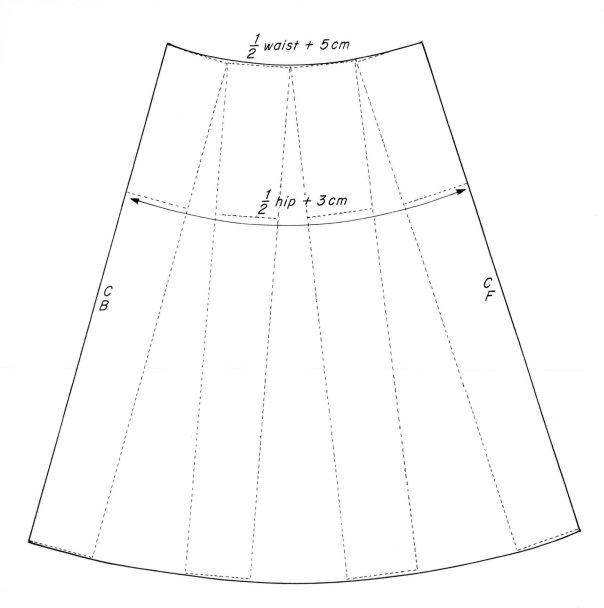

$\frac{1}{2}$ waist + 5 cm

$\frac{1}{2}$ hip + 3 cm

C
B

C
F

apart so at the hip line they measure half hip + 3 cm. The space between the strips should be equal. The easiest way to measure this curve is with a tape measure standing on its side. Pin the strips down.

6 Draw round the strips and cut the new shape out.

7 Fold the shape into two equal pieces and cut it into two.

8 Mark the left hand piece *skirt back* and the left hand edge CB which is short for *centre back*. Mark the other piece *skirt front* and the right hand edge CF.

9 The unmarked edges represent the sides of the skirt. Mark a point 2 cm in from the side seams along the waist edge. Mark a point 14 cm down the side seam from the waist edge. Join these two points with a line curving slightly into the side seam. This gives the hip shaping.

10 Mark the CB and CF with a *place to fold symbol*. Mark the pattern NET PATTERN which indicates that no seam or hem allowances have been included.

This pattern, which is straightforward, will vary in the amount of flare it gives, according to the proportions between waist, hip and length

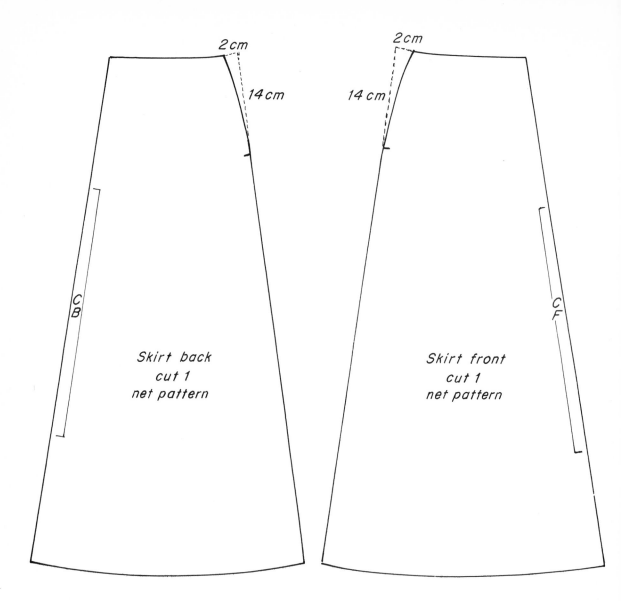

2 cm

14 cm

2 cm

14 cm

C
B

C
F

Skirt back
cut 1
net pattern

Skirt front
cut 1
net pattern

measurements of different individuals. For example, a short person with a thick waist would not have as much flare as a tall person with a slim waist.

Foundation pattern for a straight skirt

The straight skirt foundation pattern is slightly more complicated because of the darts. The first step is to take the waist, hip and length measurements. Patterns are not made to coincide exactly with the body measurements. If they were, they would be uncomfortable and would restrict the movement of the body. To overcome this, an amount is added to the body measurements during

the drawing of the foundation patterns and this is called ease allowance.

1 Draw a rectangle. The measurement across the top of the rectangle should be half the hip measurement plus 2 cm. The measurement down should be the finished length plus 1.5 cm.

2 Divide the rectangle into two equal parts lengthways and draw a line from the top to the bottom.

3 Label the left hand vertical line CB. The right hand line is labelled CF and the dividing line – side seam.

4 Shape the side seam from the waist. Mark a

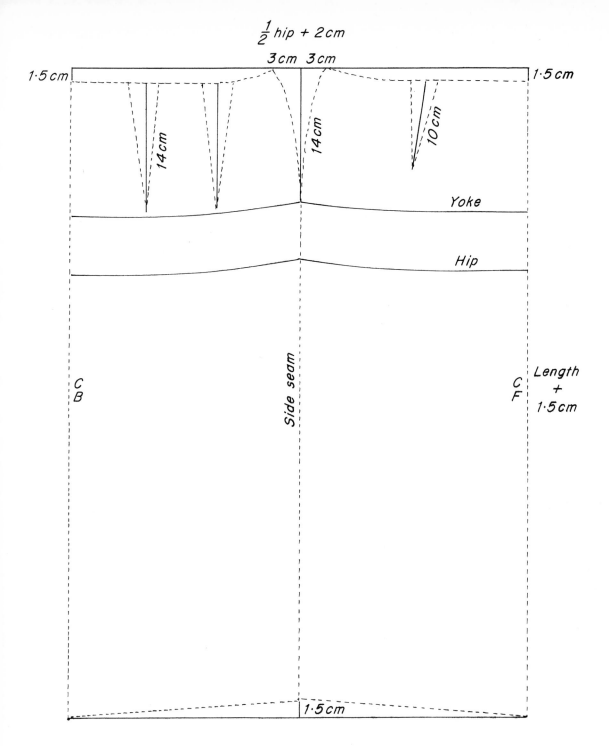

$\frac{1}{2}$ hip + 2 cm

3 cm 3 cm

1·5 cm   1·5 cm

14 cm

14 cm

10 cm

Yoke

Hip

Side seam

C
B

C
F

Length
+
1·5 cm

1·5 cm

point along the top of the rectangle 3 cm to the left of the side seam. Make a similar mark 3 cm to the right of the side seam. Draw curves from these points down the side to touch the side seam 14 cm down.

5 Shape the waist. Mark a point 1.5 cm down the

CB and the CF lines. Join these points to the side seam, curving the lines up at the sides.

6 Shape the hem. Mark a point 1.5 cm up the side seam. Draw lines from this point to base of rectangle at CB and CF.

7 Draw in these style lines: yoke line – 14 cm down from waist, hip line – 20 cm down from waist, keeping the lines parallel to the waist line.

8 Shape the waist. Stand the tape measure on its side and measure the actual waist measurement of the pattern. This will not be the same as the original half hip plus 2 cm, because of the shaping which has already been made.

9 Deduct the body waistline measurement plus 1 cm ease from the waist measurement of the pattern. The amount remaining is fullness which must be taken out in the form of darts and is referred to as the waist reduction.

Example:

	cm
Waistline measurement of pattern	46
Half body waistline measurement plus 1 cm	36
waist reduction	*10*

The number of darts needed depends on the amount of the waist reduction. The following chart of darts needed, working on the half pattern, is intended as a guide rather than a rule for dart arrangement:

Waist reduction cm	No. of darts	Position and size front cm	back cm
6	2	1 × 3	1 × 3
6.5	2	1 × 3	1 × 3.5
7	2	1 × 3.5	1 × 3.5
7.5	2	1 × 3.5	1 × 4
8	2	1 × 4	1 × 4
8.5	2	1 × 4	1 × 4.5
9	3	1 × 3	2 × 3
9.5	3	1 × 3.5	2 × 3
10	3	1 × 3	2 × 3.5
10.5	3	1 × 3.5	2 × 3.5
11	3	1 × 3	2 × 4
11.5	3	1 × 3.5	2 × 4
12	3	1 × 4	2 × 4
12.5	3	1 × 4.5	2 × 4
13	3	1 × 4	2 × 4.5
13.5	3	1 × 4.5	2 × 4.5
14	3	1 × 5	2 × 4.5

Where the waist reduction exceeds 14 cm, the amount already taken out of 3 cm to shape the waist at the side seam, can be increased by the appropriate amount.

10 Arrange the back darts. Draw two vertical lines down from the waistline extending to the yoke line. These two lines should be equally spaced across the back. Divide the amount of the back waist reduction equally between these two darts.

11 Arrange the front dart. Draw a line half-way between the side seam and the centre front seam, parallel to the side seam, extending for 10 cm. Draw the front dart on this guide line.

Before cutting out the paper pattern, fold the darts, pressing them towards the centre front or centre back. After the waist has been cut out, the dart is opened out again. The waist will have been extended to accommodate the fold of the dart.

This pattern should be cut out and made up in a piece of firmly woven fabric, such as calico. Seam allowances will have to be added first.

Pattern adjustments for fitting problems

When doubtful as to how to alter a pattern which fits badly, the first decision to be made is whether there is too much, or too little fabric covering the area. Open the seams and if necessary cut into the fabric of the skirt where it does not fit. Arrange it smoothly, either pinning out, or letting fabric in. Careful adjustment at this stage will mean carefree fitting later. Any alterations which are made to the foundation pattern in fabric must be transferred to the paper pattern.

This foundation pattern is not suitable for making up into a skirt as it has been drawn. Where the hip width and the hem are the same measurement, the finished effect would be of a skirt tighter round the hem than the hip. This pattern is used as a basis from which many variations can be developed.

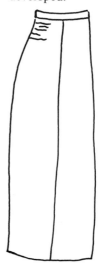
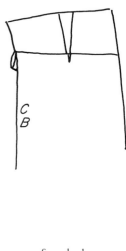

Sway back

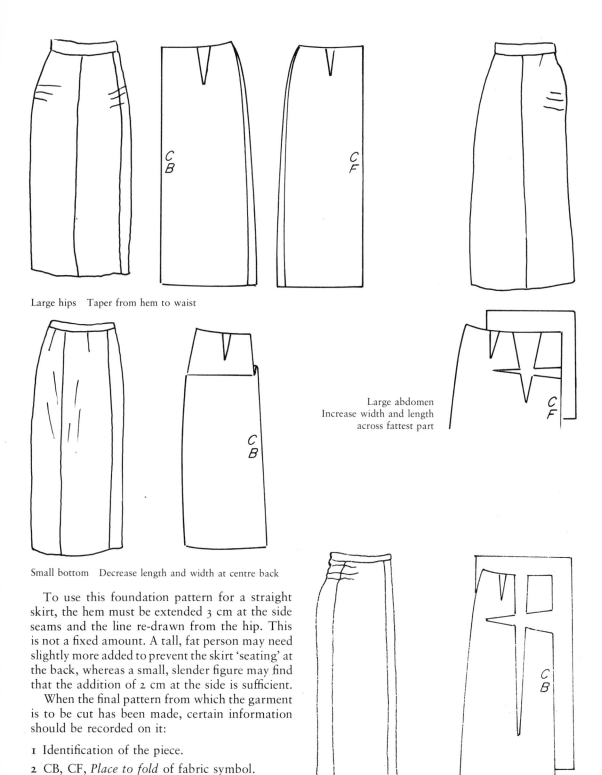

Large hips   Taper from hem to waist

Small bottom   Decrease length and width at centre back

Large abdomen
Increase width and length
across fattest part

Large bottom   Increase length and width on fattest part

To use this foundation pattern for a straight skirt, the hem must be extended 3 cm at the side seams and the line re-drawn from the hip. This is not a fixed amount. A tall, fat person may need slightly more added to prevent the skirt 'seating' at the back, whereas a small, slender figure may find that the addition of 2 cm at the side is sufficient.

When the final pattern from which the garment is to be cut has been made, certain information should be recorded on it:

1 Identification of the piece.

2 CB, CF, *Place to fold* of fabric symbol.

3 *Grain line*, this is to show how the pattern must be placed in relation to the direction in which the

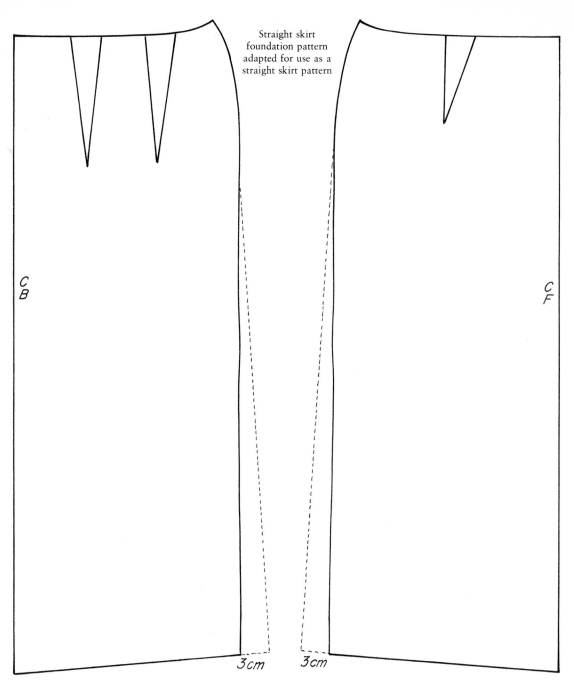

Straight skirt
foundation pattern
adapted for use as a
straight skirt pattern

C
B

C
F

3cm   3cm

woven threads of the fabric lie. The threads running parallel to the selvages are the lengthwise grain, and those which run from selvage to selvage are the crosswise grain.

4 *Balance marks*, usually called notches, are used to help accurate joining of seams, placing of panels, gathers, waist-bands.

5 *Seam allowances* can be added to the foundation pattern. The amount often used is 2 cm on all seams, and 6 cm on the hem. After tracing round the block, the allowances are added with the aid of a tape measure or gauge. Many people prefer to work with net patterns which allow the seam allowances to be planned according to the fabric,

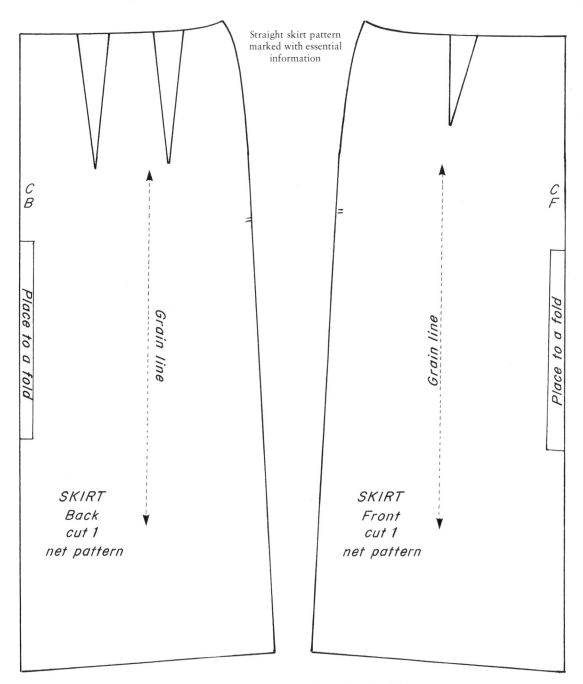

Straight skirt pattern marked with essential information

CB

Place to a fold

Grain line

SKIRT
Back
cut 1
net pattern

Grain line

CF

Place to a fold

SKIRT
Front
cut 1
net pattern

ie, perhaps wider for fraying fabrics, or narrower for sheers which will be assembled with special kinds of seams. Net patterns also make matching checks and stripes easier and, of course, any styling adaptations can be made more readily with a net pattern.

Choosing the fabric

Having created a pattern which is now ready to be made up for wear, the decision as to choice of fabric must be made. There are a great many available today. Some are made of natural fibres such as wool, linen, silk, cotton. Others are man-

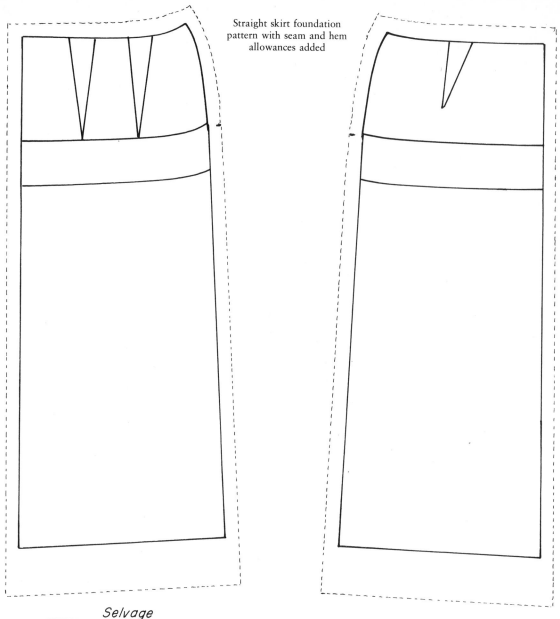

Straight skirt foundation pattern with seam and hem allowances added

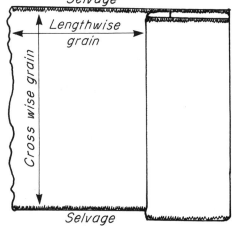

Selvage

Lengthwise grain

Cross wise grain

Selvage

made, deriving from such varied sources as wood pulp, oil and coal, and many are a combination of more than one fibre. Again, there are many ways in which these fibres can be woven or knitted to give an enormous variety of finished fabrics such as satin, tweed, lace, velvet and after that, further processes can be applied to the finished fabrics so that the problem of understanding fabrics becomes even more complex.

The questions which can be answered without a detailed knowledge of fabrics concern its weight, draping qualities, and how susceptible it is to

Checking for shrinkage

creasing. The material should be held up and if it drops into deep heavy folds, then obviously it has weight. If the fabric is held with the bias vertical to the ground, firmly woven fabric will keep its shape well and not sag. Crumple the edge of the fabric for a few seconds and see what sort of effect this has. Can the material be smoothed out fairly easily or are the creases retained?

For an A-line or straight skirt it is best to start with a smooth material which is closely woven. This will be easy to handle and will not lose its shape.

Preparing the fabric

Although most materials are pre-shrunk today, some woollens and tweeds may still shrink even during construction when the parts are pressed under a damp cloth. Where there is any doubt about the fabric, it is well to check. Outline an area 15 cm square on the fabric with a tacked line.

Press this thoroughly with a damp cloth and allow the fabric to dry. The measurements should be checked again. If there is any reduction, then the whole piece should be pressed under a damp cloth and the fabric allowed to dry before it is cut out.

If the fabric is creased it should be pressed on the wrong side, working with the grain line. It is important too, to check that a crease in material which is bought folded can be completely removed before cutting out, to avoid the danger of a permanent crease which is not part of the planned design remaining in the finished garment. Occasionally, the material is rolled on to the bolt slightly off grain and it may need pressing and pulling back into shape before cutting out.

Cutting-out

A large flat surface is needed. Many people use the dining-table, or floor, but if you sew regularly you would find that a piece of hardboard, or fibre board mounted on battens for support to lay over a smaller table is a useful investment.

Fabrics are manufactured in a variety of widths:

65 cm	127 cm
70 cm	140 cm
90 cm	150 cm
100 cm	175 cm
115 cm	180 cm
122 cm	

The width of the fabric is an important factor in deciding how the pattern pieces should be laid on the material. If it can be folded 'sideways' with a fold along one edge and the two opposite selvages along the other and the pattern laid on, this usually proves to be the most economical. If the pattern proves too wide for this, then it must be folded lengthways, with selvages at both sides. The right side should be inside, unless checks are being used, when it might be necessary to study the pattern while laying the pieces on. The pattern is then laid on, taking care to keep the grain lines

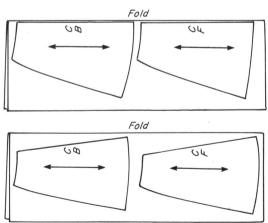
Alternative cutting layout for A-line skirt

Tracing wheel and carbon paper

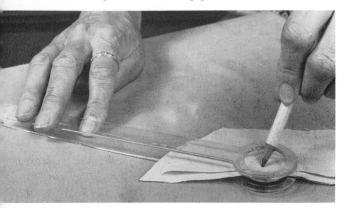
French chalk marker

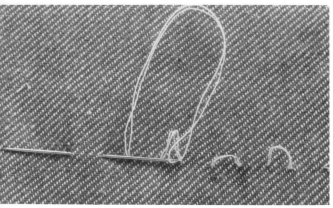
Tailors' tacks

of the fabric parallel to the grain lines marked on the pattern.

The A-line skirt may have CB and CF placed to a fold, or the grain line can be planned down the centre of the panels which will result in a 4-gore skirt with seams at CB and CF.

The straight skirt in its simplest form will have CF to a fold and CB with a seam in which the zip is fitted.

The pattern should be pinned in place with steel

pins. While putting in the pins, the material should not be lifted up, but should be kept in contact with the cutting surface. The pins should be placed round the edge, about 10 cm apart, although it is better to pin one corner, smooth the pattern and pin the opposite corner, smooth the pattern and move to an adjacent corner, to avoid the pattern buckling as it is pinned on. The pins should be put in between these points, taking care to always keep the surfaces flat and smooth. Pins should be parallel to the cutting edge and within the seam allowances.

The fabric should be kept flat on the cutting surface while cutting out with sharp, cutting-out shears. The pattern and the fabric should be held flat with one hand, while cutting out with the other. Long strokes should be used to discourage fraying the fabric. Notches should be cut outwards from the seam allowances so that they do not interfere with the seam neatening. Where the seams are going to be trimmed later they may be cut inwards, but very finely.

Before the pattern is taken off the material the information on the pattern must be transferred to the material. There are several ways of doing this, depending on the fabric.

A tracing wheel and carbon paper are useful, but this method must be checked on a piece of scrap fabric to make sure that the material is not going to be marked on the right side, or that the wheel itself will not damage the fabric. In some cases, such as tweeds, no appreciable mark can be made using this method.

The carbon paper chosen should be similar in colour to the fabric. The marking side of the carbon paper should be put next to the wrong side of the fabric, or where the material is folded to both wrong sides of the fabric. Where straight lines are to be marked it is best to run the wheel against a ruler.

Where only one layer has to be marked, french chalk is very useful and is available in a variety of colours. There is a gadget available which makes it possible to mark with french chalk where two layers are involved.

Slide the two sections of the gadget so that either the pot containing the chalk block, or the top section, are against the wrong sides of the fabric and then make a firm mark with the chalk pencil. It is quick to use, but the mark will not show on all fabrics, so it will have to be tested first.

Probably the most commonly used method is

tailors' tacks. These can be used on any kind of material and are especially useful for heavy materials, such as knobbly tweeds, and yet are also effective on sheer fabrics. It is better to use tacking cotton which has not got the silky finish of machine threads, or even strands of embroidery silk. When marking white fabrics it is safer to use white thread for the tailors' tack since although they may be slightly more difficult to locate, there will be no danger of any hint of the dye from the tacking thread marking the material.

Snipping tailors' tacks

To make tailors' tacks, use double thread and do not make a knot. A stitch is made through both thicknesses of the material. This may take the form of a single stitch through the point to be marked. Without necessarily cutting the thread, the next point which has to be marked can have a small stitch taken through all thicknesses, leaving the adjoining thread fairly loose. When all adjacent points have been marked, the joining threads are cut. The pattern can be lifted off and the two layers of fabric gently separated. The threads which lightly join the layers must be carefully snipped with sharp scissors, leaving small tufts of thread in the fabric which will remain until they are no longer needed.

Tailors' tacks in the form of small loops

Sometimes, tailors' tacks are made in the form of a loop instead of a single stitch. The loop should be less than 1 cm high and will, of course, be that much firmer than a single stitch.

Where net patterns are being used, many people prefer to mark all seam lines with tailors' tacks of the kind made by a single stitch. This makes joining the pieces very accurate and this is particularly useful for hems and essential for pleats.

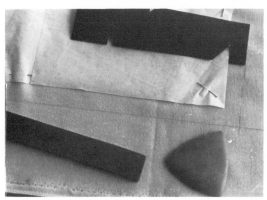

Marking seam allowances with french chalk and a cardboard gauge

Darts and guidelines such as CF and CB can be marked at the edge of the section with a tiny snip. Obviously, this quick method would not be suitable for loosely woven fabrics, or when the seam neatening is to be of the highest standard.

Where the information on the pattern to be transferred to the fabric is minimal (perhaps just two darts in the back of a skirt) it may be quicker to push a pin through the paper and both thicknesses of the material. Push another pin through from the other side, ease the pattern off and then separate the two pieces of fabric carefully, leaving the pins jutting out. The pin should be pushed through the fabric to secure it, and it should be remembered that the point where the pin first enters the fabric is the point of the dart.

Left Cutting with the grain

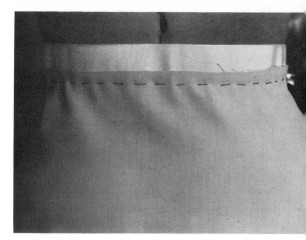

Slip tacking

Skirt with temporary waistband

Preparing for the first fitting

After the information has been transferred from the paper pattern to the fabric, the pattern pieces can be taken off as work begins on each piece. It is usual to do any construction work such as darts, tucks, pleats, zips, on separate sections before joining these into the whole skirt. Where a design is being used for the first time, or a new foundation pattern is being tried, the skirt needs to be tacked together so that it can be tried on before any permanent processes are carried out.

Tacking or basting stitches are temporary stitches which are worked usually in tacking cotton, and, except in the case of white, the colour is not important.

Certain adaptations of tacking stitches have evolved which are used according to the purpose the stitches are designed to serve.

Even tacking Here the stitches are usually about a centimetre apart and since they begin with a knot or a back stitch, they are best worked on a flat surface. The row of stitches should be finished off firmly with a back stitch. Even tacking is used to join seams which may take some strain during fitting.

Uneven tacking This is probably slightly quicker to do, but is not quite so firm and so would be more useful for attaching pockets, linings or interfacings. A long stitch is taken along the top of the fabric and one or two short stitches through the fabric.

Diagonal tacking This is sometimes called tailors' tacking and is useful for holding down pleats or other areas which lie on the surface of the skirt.

Slip tacking This is useful for joining pieces where stripes, plaids, or other patterns are to be matched. The seam allowance on one piece is tacked down and the seam line of this piece is then laid against the seam line of the piece to which it is to be joined, taking care to match the pattern while pinning the pieces together.

Tacking is done from the right side by slipping the needle through the folded edge of the top piece and then through the back of the material of the piece on which it is laid. When the whole seam has been slip tacked, the first row of tacking can be pulled out and the seam then appears to have been tacked in the usual manner.

Machine tacking Where the material is suitable, tacking can be done by machine, using the longest stitch. Some machines can be set up with a special needle which allows the machine to sew with an extra long stitch.

Fitting a skirt presents a major difficulty in that the hang of the skirt, the smoothness of the fit between the waist and the hip line, cannot be properly checked unless the skirt has a waistband. It is necessary, therefore, to fit a temporary waistband. It is useful to have a piece of petersham ribbon about 4 cm wide, which may be kept and used each time a temporary waistband is needed. It should be about 10 cm longer than the actual waist measurement which can be marked with small stitches 5 cm from each end of the petersham. The skirt may then be tacked on to this for the fitting.

A long mirror, or ideally two, is essential for judging the fit of a skirt. It should be tried on right

22

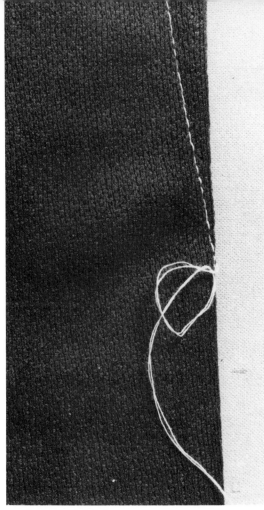

Zigzag machining

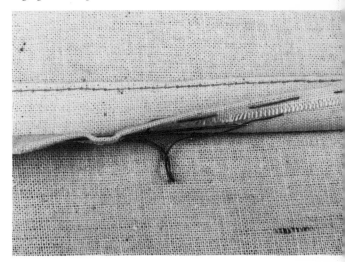

A correctly machined dart   A narrow machined edge

side out. It should hang smoothly without wrinkles or bulges. A plumb line can be used if there is any doubt. Vertical lines should be truly vertical and the hem should not dip. The skirt should be comfortable to sit and move around in and it should be flattering from all angles.

If all these criteria are fulfilled, then the construction stage has been reached. Sometimes adjustments are needed to correct minor faults. Major problems should have been overcome at the fitting of the calico version stage, but it could be that the skirt is too tight, or too loose, or the length may need some adjustment. These are factors of a design nature caused by the fact that the skirt has now been made up in fabric and the effect cannot be entirely predicted on paper.

Machining the skirt

Darts should be machined first. They should be pinned, tacked and then machined, beginning at the widest part of the dart and finishing at the point. The last two or three stitches should be made right on the edge of the fold to avoid a bulge appearing on the right side of the material. If in spite of this a dimple appears at the point of the dart on the right side, then the dart is too short and must be made longer for a smooth effect.

Side seams should be machined along the fitting line, also CB and CF seams, working from the wide end of the piece to the narrower, to eliminate fraying during construction. Before pressing any seams open, the tacking stitches should be taken out. Darts should be pressed so that the fold inclines towards the CB or CF.

If the material frays, open seams will need neatening. The most commonly used methods are by zigzag machining or by tacking and machining a narrow turning along the edge of the seam allowance. This method is suitable for medium and lightweight fabrics.

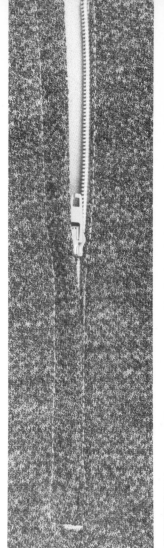

Left Opening for a zip prepared with seam allowances tacked down

Right Side back of zip machined close to zip teeth

Putting in a zip

There are several ways of putting in a zip and most people adopt or develop a method which suits them. One of the simplest is to prepare the opening in which the zip is to be fitted by tacking down the seam allowances.

With the top of the zip pinned so that it fits 3 mm below the waist seam line, the side back of the skirt is butted against the edge of the zip teeth, tacked, and then machined in place close to the teeth, using a zipper foot, or piping foot if one is available.

The front side fitting line should be laid over the zip so that the zip is completely covered. It should then be pinned, tacked and machined through all thicknesses about 1 cm from the folded edge.

The zip is sometimes machined across the bottom at an oblique angle

This method is called fitting a zip into a *lapped seam*. The other most commonly used method is in a *slot seam*. Many people find the lapped seam easier, as the problem of machining the two sides of the zip in an identical fashion is eliminated.

Left Lapped seam machined with bar tack worked across the bottom

Right Zip in a slot seam

The waistband

For the waistband, a pattern should be prepared on drafting paper.

The waistband should be cut out in fabric leaving allowances for seams. It should be pinned to the skirt right sides together, leaving the waistband extension on the skirt back and matching the fitting line of the side front to the fitting line of the waistband.

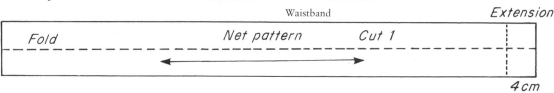

Waistband   *Extension*

Fold   *Net pattern*   *Cut 1*

4 cm

The waistband is machined to the skirt along the fitting line and across the top of the zip. The seam should be trimmed, clipped and pressed upwards. When cutting the seam allowances away to reduce bulk inside the waistband, they should be cut at different levels, the widest to the outside, to avoid a stepped effect which might be particularly noticeable in heavier fabrics. This is known as *grading*. Where interfacing is used, this should be trimmed close to the stitching.

The waistband is turned in at the ends and the raw edge turned under and hemmed to the back of the waistline machine stitches.

The hem

Finally, the hem should be turned up. The question of levelling should not be necessary in the case of the A-line or straight skirts where there are no bias seams which are likely to drop. It should be just a case of turning the skirt up along the fitting line of the hem and tacking this in place about 1 cm from the turned edge. The raw edge of the hem needs to be dealt with before it is sewn up so that it will not fray. If the side seams have been zigzagged or stitched with a narrow turning, the raw edge of the hem may be treated in the same way.

The hem should be tacked again 5 mm from the neatened edge which can then be blind hemmed into position.

Hooks and bars attached with blanket stitch

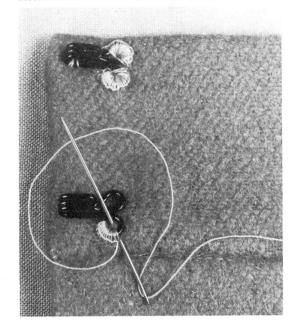

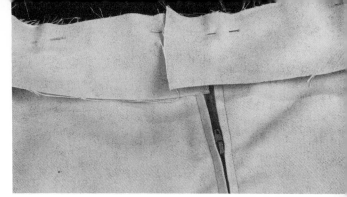

Waistband pinned to right side of skirt

Graded seam allowances

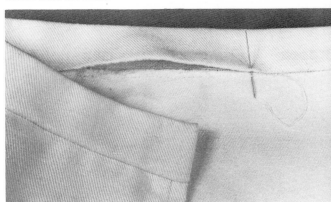

Waistband turned under and hemmed

Blind hemming

Design

The selection of essentials

Although elements of design are limited and the human shape is fairly standard, the problem of achieving the most agreeable effect can prove difficult. This sometimes becomes easier after a close look at the factors involved.

The choice of the design and the fabric depend on each other. If the skirt has soft folds, then it could not be interpreted in a crisp fabric. The design must relate to the fabric. Plain fabrics can be darted without restriction, whereas a design motif might be spoiled by darts and the subsequent distribution of fullness which would have to be planned. Diagonal stripes which are distorted by darts would have to have fullness moved to the side seams, or be controlled by gathers or tucks.

A design might concentrate on fabric with simple lines, or the effect may depend on decoration, pockets, braid, embroidery. There are no absolute rules about combining textures, colours and designs. Invention often over-rules tradition. Different personalities approach the problem from different angles. The adventurous can make mistakes, but can also look stunning, whereas the more traditional will perhaps look unfailingly elegant.

It is impossible to say which should come first, the style or the fabric. Sometimes it will be one, sometimes the other, but as soon as one is chosen, then limitations are placed on the choice of the other. For example, a draped style must be carried out in a fabric which has draping qualities.

Ideas for designs are not hard to find, but some people need to make a conscious effort to use their eyes when looking at magazines, fashion reports, shop windows or other people's clothes. The silhouette, proportions, style lines and any special features should be looked at carefully. It might be possible to detect where the shaping is, what darts there are and decide whether any seams conceal

Skirt with soft folds

Diagonal fabric spoilt by darting

Draped

dart control. Decoration should be studied. Are there any dart tucks, pleats, gathers, shirring, smocking? Where are the style lines located in relation to yoke, hip and knee? Where is the straight grain? Is the skirt bias cut? What sort of top is being worn? Does the outfit disguise or emphasise any figure faults?

Would a particular design be personally flattering, or would adjustments have to be made to the skirt, the top or the accessories before it would be right?

The analysis of design can be distilled even further. The elements are colour, texture and line. Keeping this simple statement in mind is helpful. Looking at an outfit gives an impression which might be pleasing, or not. The next step is to decide why such an effect has been created. This is where referring to the elements mentioned above might help. Is it the colour or colour scheme which has succeeded? Is it the right line and proportion for the figure of the person wearing it? Has the whole outfit been created in fabrics of appropriate textures? If the answer to these questions is yes, then the effect must be pleasing. If the outfit looks unattractive which of these elements is wrong? It could, of course, be all of them.

Colour

Often the first thing which is noticed first about clothes is the colour. The primary colours are red, yellow and blue and any of these colours mixed together produce the secondary colours, purple, orange and green. Further combinations of these basic six colours are extended by the addition of white or black to create an infinite range of shades.

Colours can give an impression of warmth; red and orange and sometimes yellow do this, whereas blue and green and white appear cool. Dark colours on the whole seem warmer. Some colours impose as they appear to be closer, red and yellow are often in this category together with light, bright colours, whereas some shades of blue appear to recede. These are all optical illusions and yet are facts which cannot be ignored when considering fashion, complementing existing wardrobe colours, or building up a colour scheme from a basic colour.

A wide range of different colour schemes is possible. Monochromatic schemes will use various shades of one colour, or one colour with black and white. Other schemes rely on colours which are closely related for a harmonious effect,

such as blue with turquoise and green, or yellow with orange and red. A scheme which involves the use of opposite colours such as red and green, purple and orange would create a bold and dramatic effect. An interesting problem emerges in deciding the amounts of each colour to use in relation to the other and the intensity of each colour. Should one be light and the other dark, and which should predominate?

Colour can affect mood. Some colours are cheerful and aggressive and others cool and serene, and within each colour different shades have different effects. Skirts in basic plain colours, brown, dark blue, grey, have useful lives coordinating with a wardrobe of blouses, sweaters and jackets, while bright skirts in rich patterns add drama and gaiety to an outfit. Bright colours, scarves and waistcoats with a plain grey sweater and skirt will flatter most figures and ages.

A large area is often best reserved for a more subdued colour and the bright colours can be most effective in small areas such as scarves, belts, pockets, or even pocket bindings. Very interesting effects are often produced by using variations in tone or a similar colour for pockets, pleat backings, binding. For contrast, a deeper shade of the main colour is effective applied to a hem or for trimming. Repetition of colours gives a harmonious effect. The yoke of a blouse can be made of the same material as the skirt and this will give a unified effect and yet not necessarily restrict the use of either garment.

Patterns are colour combinations and most will have a dominant colour which must be considered when working out accessories to wear with skirts. The size of the wearer cannot be ignored when considering patterns but the top and skirt outfit gives scope for wearing bright, bold patterns which might be best avoided in dresses. A plain top in a basic colour, perhaps black, makes it possible to wear prints for a flared skirt or wraparound skirt which could not, for very big people perhaps, be worn in any other way.

Long straight skirts too, can be worn in vivid prints, rich brocades and sequinned fabrics which might otherwise overwhelm the wearer.

Colour schemes are affected by the overall social climate. Whether the mood of the times is romantic, optimistic or austere has a great deal of influence.

Often a personal colour scheme evolves without any deliberate planning. Personal taste and fashion, influencing each purchase, cause many

Plain top and patterned skirt

people to develop a co-ordinating wardrobe without making any conscious effort.

It might prove necessary, on the other hand, for a less colour-conscious person to decide carefully on the colours which are most flattering and to deliberately follow a policy of keeping a colour scheme in mind when shopping. The colour of a person's eyes sometimes gives a clue here. Often there is a fleck of colour in the iris of an eye which, although insignificant, might prove a very flattering colour to wear. Looking at nature provides an infinite variety of colour combinations: the violet and green of the African Violet, the rich, warm reds and browns of autumn could provide the starting point for the development of a colour scheme.

Basic colours are usually darker and are used for major wardrobe items, such as coats, suits or skirts. These should be of very good quality material which would be expected to have a useful life of several years. The colours should not be imposing, but should lend themselves to change with the addition of contrasting or complementary colours for less expensive items. When choos-

ing blouses, sweaters, shoes, bags, fabric for skirts, if the basic wardrobe colour is kept in mind, an interchangeable wardrobe will develop which is useful and economical.

In the world of fashion a colour emerges each season which illustrates the mood of the season. Variations on that colour will be seen in magazines and shop windows where fashion clothes are displayed. A wardrobe which has skirts in basic colours and lines will easily adapt to the introduction of new colours in the form of blouses, jackets, waistcoats or scarves.

Texture

In addition to colour, texture is an important feature of trends in fashion. The texture not only involves the appearance of the fabric, its sheen or dullness, roughness or smoothness, but also its weight, the draping qualities and the richness or plainness of the effect.

Developing skill in fabric selection is not easy. The fabric must not only look good, but it must also be of the right weight and have the necessary draping qualities for a design. Will the fabric hold pleats? Is it firm enough to retain its shape? Experience is the best teacher and this is gained by feeling fabrics, looking at fabrics used in skirts already made-up, and reading and noting the kinds of fabrics described in books and magazines as being suitable for use in particular styles. Generalisations emerge: soft crêpes and shiny satins are feminine; whereas smooth, firmly woven gaberdines and worsteds are often chosen for tailored skirts and tweeds are effective for tailored or softer styles.

Line

Lines create illusion. Several lines are involved in any outfit: the lines of the body, the lines of the clothes and the lines on the clothes in the form of seams, shapes and decoration.

Certain guiding principles can be accepted which help in the initial consideration of good lines. Vertical lines can give a taller and thinner effect by leading the eye in an up and down direction. Horizontal lines across a figure fault should be avoided as they are lines which attract the eye most strongly. Lines may be straight or curved. Curved lines are easier to wear and softer than straight lines. They are more romantic, soft and pretty. Short diagonal lines give the impression of width, whereas longer diagonal lines give a longer, narrower look.

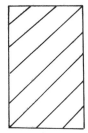 

Straight lines seem stiff, disciplined, strict, but direction plays its part: vertical lines may be considered regal, elegant; horizontal lines serene; level, smooth and diagonal lines more relaxed and casual.

A skirt needs to be considered, of course, as part of a whole and this fact relates to the question of proportion. A top and a skirt must together create an attractive effect which is in proportion to the whole figure. The length of the skirt must be considered, not only in the light of current fashion, but also in relation to the shoes and top which will generally be worn with it. The position of trim-

Vertical lines on a skirt

Horizontal lines
on a skirt

mings as well as style and design lines affect the balance of the skirt. The rules of today will generally be broken tomorrow and where once we might be told *never* to wear a full skirt with a blouson top, another time this would give a top fashion silhouette. There can therefore be no strict rules. Awareness of fashion, careful scrutiny of personal proportions, concern for wardrobe from the view of life-style, age, personality, are the important factors. Consider the total look and be prepared to make adjustments in length, fit and arrangement of decoration to achieve the most attractive effect.

Fabrics

Until quite recently all fabrics were made from wool, cotton, silk, or linen fibres and these four natural fibres have distinctive qualities. The number of fibres available has now been extended by the addition of a wide range of synthetic or man-made fibres, whose origins are cellulosic, regenerated protein, or chemical. The range is wide, the processes are complex, and the resulting names are often difficult to remember or even in some cases, pronounce. These fibres, too, have their particular characteristics.

The properties of natural fibres are still unmatched, as for example the warmth of wool, the absorbency of cotton and linen and the lustre of silk. Man-made fabrics are generally easy to work with and easy to care for, although if they are not specially treated they may create static electricity and attract dirt. However, fabrics which combine fibres from both groups often offer the best of both worlds. Cotton and polyester fabrics have the coolness and absorbency of cotton, combined with the strength and crease-shedding qualities of polyester.

The important advantage which exists in knowing the fibre content of a fabric is in the different handling which might be needed during making-up and its care in wear. Awareness of the problems and sensible precautions should prevent any disasters occurring. The questions which arise are: How does the fabric respond to heat? How should it be pressed? Will it shrink? Can it be washed? Will a special needle be needed for the machine to avoid puckering? These questions should be asked when the material is bought, but if there is any doubt that the answers might not be correct, the safe way is to double check.

Check for shrinkage by pressing with a damp cloth. Check if a hot iron damages the fibres by trying a hot iron on the wrong side and the right side of the fabric. Some man-made fabrics can be spoiled by ironing with a hot iron and a warm iron must be used on the wrong side throughout construction. Wash a small piece and compare it with a test piece cut in a similar size. Machine a small scrap where there is any doubt about the sewing machine needle, and if any puckering occurs, it will be necessary to use a ballpoint sewing machine needle which pushes between the threads rather than piercing them.

The discussion concerning what a fabric is made of leads on to the question of what has been made from it. By a process of either weaving or knitting a piece of material of quite distinctive characteristics may be produced. Many fabrics such as velvet or tweed, for example, can have practically identical counterparts which are made from yarns of completely different origins and therefore possibly needing different handling.

There is a rich vocabulary of fabric names describing an infinite variety of textures. The important thing about fabrics, from a dressmaking point of view, is their suitability for the successful interpretation of a design.

Skirts are often made from heavier materials such as woollens, linen, cotton and terylene in the less full styles. Straight skirts are not usually successful when made up in a flimsy fabric. The fabric should be handled. Is it heavy? The weave should be examined for closeness and evenness. It should be pulled in the direction of the warp and weft to gauge the firmness. Pleats need a firm, even weave. Some twill weaves resist pleating and are better left for flares. Jersey and double knit fabrics are suitable for flared skirts, as well as panelled and unpressed pleat styles.

How does the fabric look? It may have a silky textured finish, such as crêpe-de-chine, or be sheer, like chiffon which gathers and drapes well. It might look rich like brocade, or lacy. Cotton or linen-look fabrics are usually firm and are heavy, or lightweight, according to how they have been woven. Woollens, tweeds and knitted fabrics are especially useful for skirt-making. In temperate climates they are warm in winter and comfortable in summer.

Further complications arise even after coming to terms with the fibre content of a fabric, how it handles and its appearance. Finishes which include crease-resistance, machine washability or lustre may be given to the fabric. These should be made evident when the material is bought, but will become recognizable with the aid of detective work and experience.

Skirt design

Once a fashion shape is accepted, the variations in cut to achieve this line are quite wide ranging. Of course, a good line is the most distinctive feature of a well-cut skirt. From the criteria of fit nothing is as important as the line, that is, the way it hangs and the outline or silhouette it gives to the figure.

A skirt may be straight from waist to hem and tighter at the hem than round the hips. It may be A-line, that is, following the natural line of the body when walking and widening a little towards the hem. It may be bell-shaped or flared from the waist, producing a full hem.

All commercial patternmakers produce skirt designs in their catalogues. Many are classic styles which remain favourites year after year, while others reflect current trends. Sometimes, however, a particular effect is wanted which cannot be found in the catalogues. Sometimes personal measurements vary widely from the standard

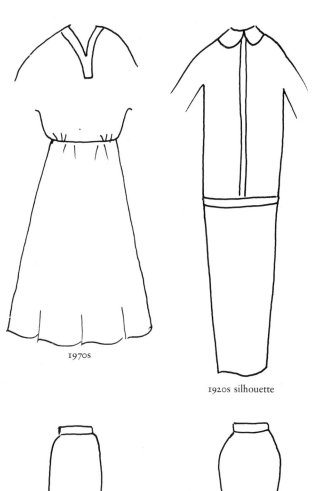

1970s

1920s silhouette

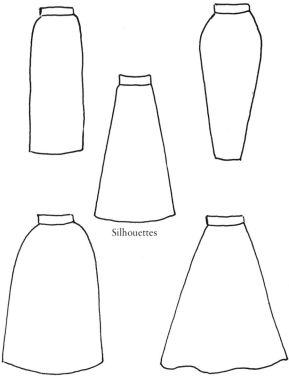

Silhouettes

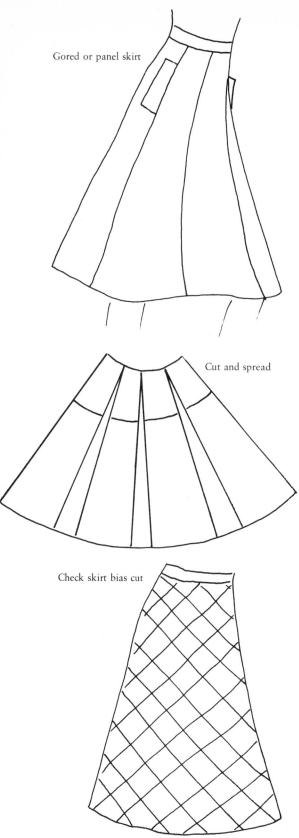

Gored or panel skirt

Cut and spread

Check skirt bias cut

measurements used when making these patterns and some people enjoy experimenting and developing their own personal ideas. Each of these factors provides a good case for understanding pattern construction and adaptation.

A rectangle can be developed into a pattern by reducing width at the top and increasing width at the hem. Any of the steps in the development of a shape, from a rectangle to a circle, can be used as a foundation pattern. To bring this variety into some order, several lines can be isolated and then a particular design can be looked at in relation to these.

The straight skirt, a self-explanatory shape, is often used for draped styles. The A-line is very popular, particularly lending itself to outfits where longer tops are to be worn, such as tailored jackets and below-the-waist sporty tops. It is also a very easy to wear line. The fully shaped skirt fits neatly round the hips but has more fullness in the hem and no darts at the waist. The line of the fully shaped skirt will vary for different figures, according to individual measurements, ie the difference between the waist and the hips. The smaller the waist is in proportion to the hips, the more fullness there is to be transferred into the hem. A person with a small waist will have a skirt which will be fuller in the hem.

The construction of the slightly flared skirt is different to the first three mentioned. It has more fullness at the hip and the skirt hem is almost a semi-circle. The fully flared skirt is a full circle. Only the waist measurement of the skirt matches the body measurement in these two shapes.

To interpret a design it is necessary to assess the amount of fullness to be brought into the hemline and this is mainly a matter of judgement which develops with experience. When possible measure hems and note the effect in relation to waist, hip and length.

A design must first of all be considered according to its silhouette in relation to these shapes. The one which is nearest can be used as a starting point. From here more or less flare may be taken into account, after which further design details are worked out.

The simplest designing of skirt styles involves the division of the foundation pattern into gores or panels. Some foundation patterns are most suitable for styles with many gores. They are sometimes of four, eight or sixteen gores, although six, twelve and ten are also quite often used.

Extra fullness can be added between the gores in the form of flares, godets and pleats. Basically, fullness is added by cutting up the pattern and introducing extra width where it is wanted. Flares appear as the result of making a piece of material hang in such a way that one of its edges develops fullness, while the opposite edge remains quite flat without gathers or pleats. Flares appear in hems and other parts of skirts as frills and loose panels. A flared frill fitted onto the skirt would be made by outlining the area on the skirt pattern which is traced through to another piece of paper and cut out. This piece of pattern must be folded, cut and spread evenly to form the flares. Any skirt pattern can be cut and spread to produce flares.

Skirt designs are sometimes created by pleating, gathering or draping a piece of fabric to fit the figure. A rectangle is most suitable where there is extra fullness throughout the length, ie in pleated or gathered skirts. There are no fixed allowances for these skirts and the amount allowed over the body measurements depends on the fabric and the line wanted.

Pleats may be straight, or shaped. Folds or tucks may form at the waistband without the fullness being carried through to the hem. Gathered skirts may be straight or shaped, narrow or full at the hem. Where a great deal of fullness is wanted at the hem, a shaped foundation pattern is more suitable as it reduces the bulk at the waistline. The fully shaped skirt block used twice makes a good gathered skirt. Gathers, too, might be introduced in sections, as gathered panels which might be straight or shaped.

The hang of the skirt is partly governed by the grain of the fabric. Sometimes, for a special effect, a garment is cut on the horizontal grain, or sometimes for decorative reasons, fabric is used on the bias. The bias used down the centre front of a skirt produces a moulded, clinging fit and is often used for draped effects.

The addition of hip yokes is useful as it not only widens the range of styles, but can camouflage figure faults. If the line of the hip yoke is carefully placed, it can be used for gathered or pleated styles which would be unattractive where a figure has a thick waist or abdomen. A deeper yoke would draw attention to a slim waist and away from heavy hips and buttocks.

Craftsmanship

A skirt will progress from a foundation pattern through any number of stages, depending on the complexity of the design, to a final garment. In the early stages, curves may have become distorted by cutting and spreading sections of the pattern, and must be corrected to fit the shape of the body. Darts may have to be shortened to soften the effect and give more ease. Individual dressmaking techniques add interest with embroidery and other forms of decoration which would make the cost of a ready-made skirt prohibitive. Seams can be highlighted with top stitching, and insertions, piping, belts, bands, pockets and welts are all attractive additions.

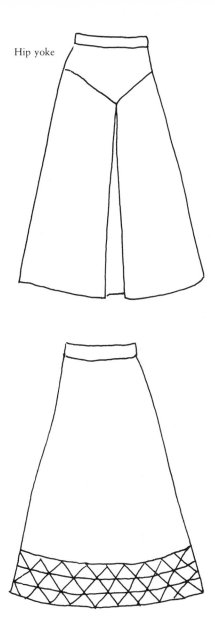

Hip yoke

Many people have found that with few exceptions home-made clothes are more hardwearing than manufactured ones, because they can combine good design, perfect fit and good craftsmanship.

Good craftsmanship begins with the right approach. The most suitable equipment must be available as well as space in which to work. Initially it might be found that working to a high standard of craftsmanship is time-consuming, but eventually it will be found that working the right way is the quick way.

Equipment can be stored in a box or a cupboard but must include:

Scissors for cutting paper
Small scissors for cutting threads, notches
Sharp cutting-out scissors

Tacking cotton
Machine cotton to match the work in hand
Embroidery threads – never throw any away

Needles for hand sewing
Sewing machine needles – assorted sizes and ballpoint for difficult fabrics

A tape measure
Tracing wheel and carbon paper
Pins and pin cushion

Large items are the sewing machine, an iron and ironing board, and a full-length mirror.

The measuring tools needed for pattern drafting have been listed and most dressmakers find, as their interest develops and experience grows, that other sewing aids will gradually be acquired.

Working space is often a problem. This can be solved by reserving a drawer or cupboard for storage, and having a large piece of chipboard at least 1 metre wide by 2 metres long, mounted on battens which can be placed over a smaller table for pattern drafting or cutting-out. This can obviously be taken off and stored vertically when it is not being used.

Figure types

A carefully scrutinised figure check is essential and this, combined with accurate measurements, should reveal the true situation. Standard measurements based on average proportions require the bust to be 5 cm smaller than the hip. The waist is 20 cm smaller than the hip in the larger sizes, ranging down to 25 cm smaller than the hip in the smaller sizes. Heaviness often develops at the waist, abdomen, buttocks or thighs. A hollow

back below the waistline is often referred to as a *sway back*.

Choosing a skirt pattern which will fit non-standard measurements depends on the style. Straight skirt patterns and designs which develop from straight skirts, such as draped and pleated styles, are best chosen according to the nearest hip measurement. All flared styles are best chosen according to the waist measurement, although if the variation is more than 8 cm, it is as well to put the tape measure across the hip line of the pattern to make sure that the style and ease allowances will accommodate the difference.

Fullness which may be in the form of gathers, shirring or pleats must be given some thought. It is usually disastrous for this to develop at the thickest part of the body, whether it is at waist or hip. If it is planned 10 cm or so above or below the thickest part, the more fitting parts of the skirt will be where the body is thinner.

Finding a flattering skirt style is perhaps most difficult for thick-waisted figures, as this is a point at which the skirt must fit. The most difficult style is the all-round gathered skirt. Possible solutions are by keeping to heavier materials which will hang well, using soft folds rather than gathers, or putting the gathers on a hip yoke. It is safer to keep to straight, A-line, or fully shaped silhouettes, incorporating design detail in the form of pleats and gathered panels at centre front, or centre back. The most satisfactory solution is to combine skirts with blouses and jackets which will fit over the top of the skirt waist about 8 cm below the waistline.

A prominent abdomen should not be emphasized with fullness either, and where a style is wanted with fullness from the waist, it is better to keep gathering to the sides of the skirt, with the front panel smooth. A-line and flared silhouettes are useful, but if the problem is serious, hip-length jackets or blouses worn with slender skirts look very flattering.

Where the figure problem is thick hips or thighs, flowing lines from the waist in the form of box pleats, flares and gathers are a very successful camouflage. A straight skirt is more difficult. It should be fitted carefully to make sure that there is sufficient ease allowance over the broadest parts. A dark or neutral colour with smooth, fine fabrics will not draw attention to the area. Attractive tops will draw the eye and contrast with plain skirts whose features are good material, well-cut and beautifully made. At the other end of the skirt,

Blouson, flattery for a thick waist

pattern, colour and decoration at the hem line are effective in emphasising pretty legs.

The problem of course can also be one of too little! Slim people can look most feminine in skirts gathered at the waist and any other skirt style. The term, *small* in height is usually reserved for people who are 1.60 m or less and here care is needed. Contrasting top and skirt outfits are not usually flattering. One-colour or monochromatic schemes are more effective, particularly in respect of the short and stout. Dark and medium colours will make a heavy figure appear taller and thinner, and light, bright colours with marked contrasts are best avoided. The trend should be to plain fabrics. The vertical line illusion should be used, giving favour to pleats and avoiding wide belts with short skirts.

The effect of stripes can vary considerably, as it depends on the distance between the stripes and the widths of the stripes. The only sure way to gauge the effect of a fabric is to stand in front of the mirror with the fabric draped across the body.

It is worthwhile experimenting with combinations. Often the most unexpected succeeds and using skirts and tops gives a wide scope for trying out new ideas and testing different effects.

Fashion

Fashion is strictly contemporary, reflecting current moods. Within each fashion a wide range of choice exists. Although styles in clothes may appear to change quickly, beneath the apparent dramatic changes reported after the collections shown by the leading fashion designers, in fact the changes are gradual, and are influenced by the social or political climate, they are perhaps ideological or spin-offs from the entertainment world. For example, the 'New Look' of 1946 echoed the movement forward into the 'new' future, away from the anxieties and austerities of the years of war. The hippies adopted a uniform which filtered through the design world leaving its mark in a trend both romantic and individualistic.

35

Tennis skirt

New look 1947 –
length from the ground
from 40 cm to 24 cm

Gimmicks and tricks too, are part of fashion and add fun and variety to what could become an over-solemn part of life.

Fashion is communal, but is interpreted at a highly individual level. Home dressmakers have a much greater opportunity to adapt fashion trends to their personal ideas and needs.

Wardrobe planning

What kind of skirts are needed in a wardrobe? When will they be worn? What time of the year? What styles are the most flattering? What about fabrics? Is it necessary to choose washable fabrics which will stand heavy wear and remain uncrushed?

The answers to these questions are the beginning of wardrobe planning because they start to analyse the essentials to consider. Life-style plays an important part in finding the answers.

At home, flared A-line skirts which are washable are useful when coping with housework and caring for a family. Two or three simple skirts in a denim corduroy which can be washed through after a day or two of wear can be useful throughout most of the year and will look attractive with T-shirt tops or more elaborate blouses to ring the changes.

Career girls appear to favour a more tailored line, uncluttered, in basic colours, often dark. There is economy here in that changes can be made by using different tops, sweaters and jackets and many skirts can be worn throughout the year with tops chosen according to the weather.

Flared skirts are comfortable for travelling and in a man-made fabric, or a natural and man-made mixture, retain a fresh appearance throughout a long journey.

Many sports require a certain type of clothing and short, flared or pleated skirts in appropriate colours are worn for tennis, badminton and skating. Wraparound skirts are useful for sportswear since they are so very comfortable as the fit can be adjusted according to any slight variation in waist measurements. They are useful too, to accompany beachwear, as it looks more attractive to unwrap a skirt, rather than wriggle in, or out of it.

Of course, the top which will be worn with the skirt must be given a great deal of thought too. The versatility of a skirt is obvious as it can be worn with anything from a T-shirt to an evening blouse. Plain or patterned tops, a timeless shirt, or a high-fashion, one-season blouse, sporting windcheater, or tailored jacket; each must be considered in relation to the wearer for the effect it creates, with an eye open for modification where the finished effect is not quite right.

Skirt patterns

There are some fortunate people whose body measurements match those standardized by paper pattern manufacturers. They can therefore avoid having to make a basic foundation pattern for themselves and, by making a few minor adjustments to the ready-made pattern, can bring it totally into line with their own individual measurements.

A foundation pattern is one which is cut from either standard or body measurements. Although it includes ease allowance and shaping, it has no design fullness or trimming. Usually no seam allowances are included. It can be used to make plain skirts, or as a basis for creating more intricate designs.

For the many whose proportions vary considerably from the standard, it may well prove an economy in time and effort to tackle the mathematics of constructing foundation patterns which can be used again and again, secure in the knowledge that a good fit will be obtained.

With practice, pattern-making gets progressively easier. At first, without any other help except that which is offered in this book it may appear somewhat difficult to construct a straight skirt foundation pattern. However, by persevering and devoting some time particularly to sketching and planning skirts in small scale this will soon lead to an ability to analyse the line of a skirt and devise an approach to the creation of a design.

Initially it is quite a good idea to work out a design using a small scale, such as quarter, fifth or even a sixth and the graduated set squares and rulers make this very simple.

To guarantee a perfect fit, a foundation pattern whether drafted to personal measurements or bought ready-made, should be made up in calico or some other firm, inexpensive fabric. It should be fitted with a temporary waistband and studied carefully. Does it fit smoothly without pulling or wrinkling? Is there too much fullness at any point? Is extra width needed to allow for a large abdomen or heavy thighs? If the seams do not hang vertically, the skirt needs lifting at the waist at either the back or the front.

The line of a skirt is the overall shape and the way it hangs. This ranges from a skirt which appears to be tighter round the hem than round the hips (a style popular some time ago known as the hobble skirt) through a seemingly straight skirt, to one which follows the natural line of the body, now commonly known as A-line, to an increasingly full hemline which may be in excess of a complete circle. The amount of width added to the hem of the skirt decides the line.

Five different lines have been selected for which foundation patterns are described. It is easier to become familiar with these so that when looking at a design and attempting to create a pattern for it, the foundation pattern which is nearest to it in line can be used as a starting point, after which more or less fullness might need to be added.

The straight skirt foundation pattern has already been described. This is developed into the A-line and then the fully shaped skirts. The slightly flared and fully flared skirts are made in a different way and the amount of fullness wanted at the hem is easily adjusted.

The examples illustrated are based on the standard size 14; hip 97 cm, waist 71 cm, length 69 cm, with the hip 20 cm down from the waist. Where personal measurements vary considerably from standard measurements, the line of the foundation pattern might not be completely comparable with that made from standard measurements. This applies particularly to the fully shaped foundation pattern. This means that when interpreting a design, a more or less flared foundation pattern would be used for the starting point.

Any information which will be needed during cutting out and making up should be marked on the finished pattern. Notches help in the putting together of the various pieces of a garment and they are shown by crossed lines in the basic

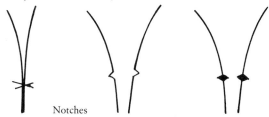

Notches

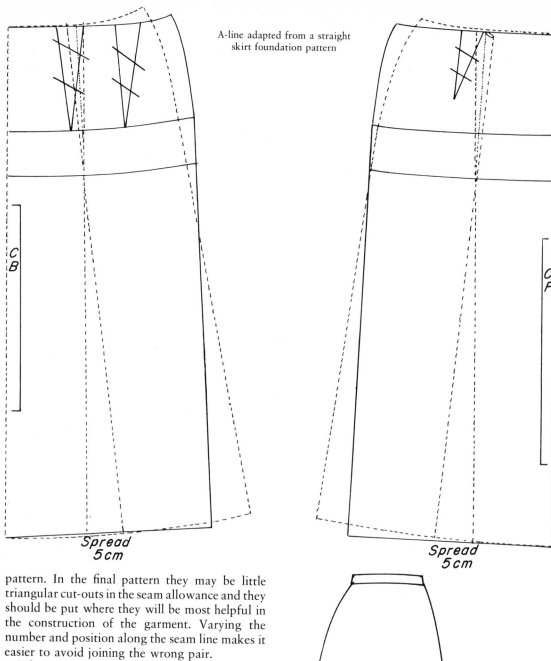

A-line adapted from a straight
skirt foundation pattern

C
B

Spread
5 cm

C
F

Spread
5 cm

pattern. In the final pattern they may be little triangular cut-outs in the seam allowance and they should be put where they will be most helpful in the construction of the garment. Varying the number and position along the seam line makes it easier to avoid joining the wrong pair.

When cutting the notches in fabric it is easier to cut into the seam allowance, making a very small snip, but where the fabric frays, or the seam allowance needs to be kept intact for neatening, a small triangular shape should be cut outwards.

Adapting the straight skirt foundation pattern to a slightly shaped or A-line style

1 Draw round or trace the straight skirt pattern.

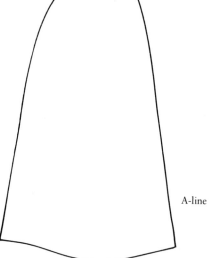

A-line

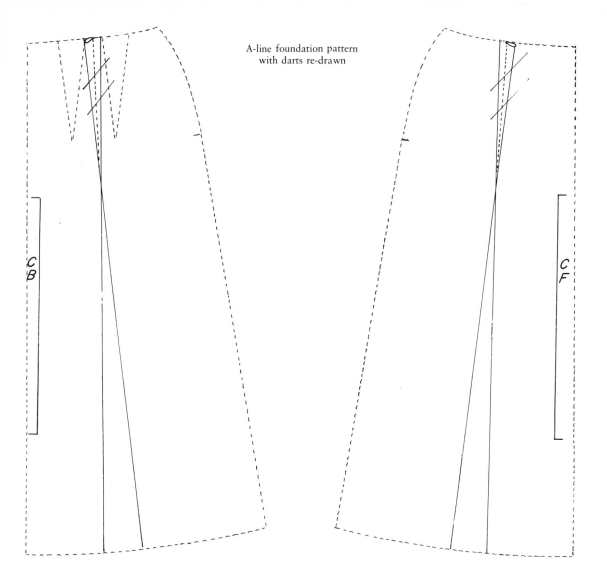

A-line foundation pattern
with darts re-drawn

*C
B*

*C
F*

2 Re-plan the darts so that the waist reduction is equally divided between the front and back pieces. Draw a vertical line from the waist to the hip, half-way between CF or CB and side seam and draw the darts.

3 Continue the vertical line to the hem.

4 Cut up the vertical line from the hem to the hip line and spread the pattern for 5 cm at the hem.

5 This will reduce the amount to be included in the darts which must now be re-drawn. In the size 14 example the waist reduction becomes 6 cm, it was 10 cm before. This means that the front dart can now be left out and two back darts drawn from waist to yoke line, each of 3 cm.

Adapting the straight skirt foundation pattern to a fully shaped skirt which has a fitted waist and hip with maximum fullness at the hem

This line is similar to the one produced by the easy flared skirt pattern described in chapter 1.

1 Draw round or trace the straight skirt foundation pattern.

2 Re-arrange the darts so that the waist reduction is equally divided between the front and back pieces (in the same way that the pattern was adapted for the A-line skirt) along a vertical line from the waist to the hip, halfway between the CB and the side seam.

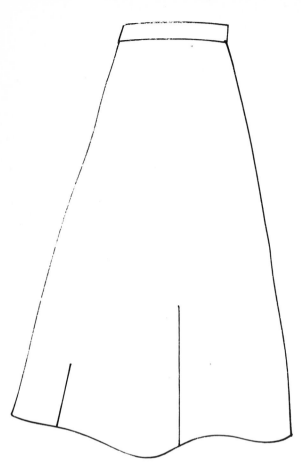

Fully shaped skirt

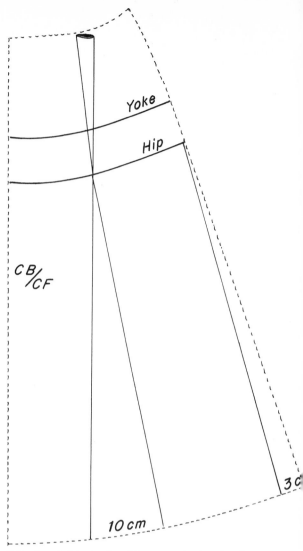

Fully shaped skirt developed from straight skirt foundation pattern. Front and back similar shapes

3 Fold in the dart half way between the CB and side seam, slashing it up from the hem to the base of the dart. Allow the slash to spread so that the dart lies quite flat. In the example the space at the hem is 10 cm.

4 Extend the hem for 3 cm at the side and re-draw the side seam from the hip. This line should be the same length as the original side seam, which will keep the curve of the hem correct.

The back and front pieces are identical shapes and no darts are necessary.

Slightly flared skirt

1 Draw a rectangle the length of the skirt × half waist measurement.

2 Draw in the hip line 20 cm down from the waist

3 Fold the rectangle in half, and then in quarters, this will divide it into four equal strips. Cut the rectangle into separate strips.

4 Lay the strips on another sheet of paper. Keep the pieces touching at the waist line and spread them equally so that at the hem an area of nearly a quarter of a circle is completed. Check that at the hips the measurement is more than half the hips plus 2 cm.

5 Draw the curves smoothly.

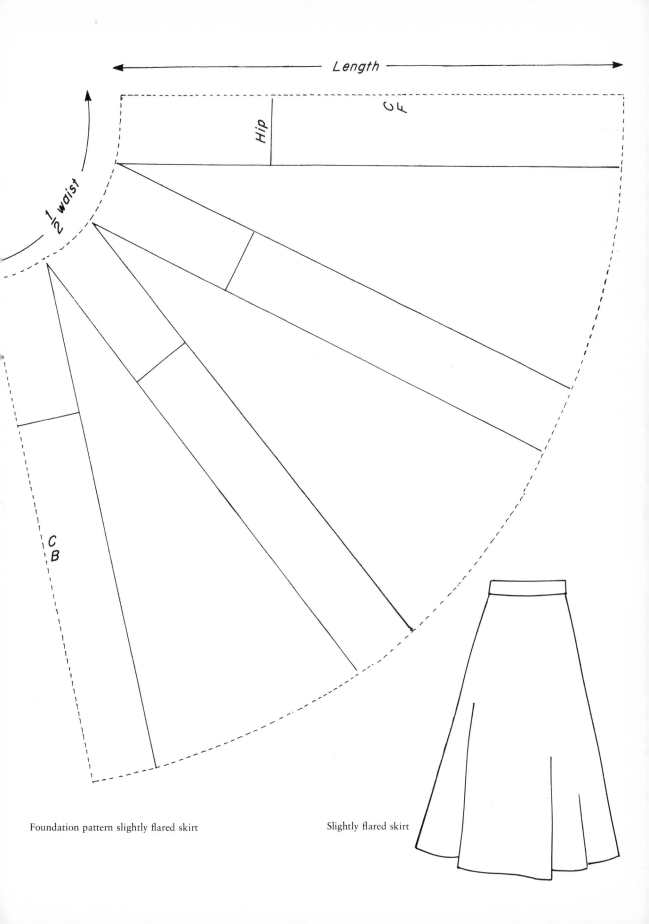

Length

CF

Hip

$\frac{1}{2}$ waist

CB

Foundation pattern slightly flared skirt

Slightly flared skirt

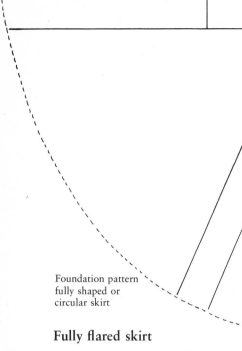

Foundation pattern
fully shaped or
circular skirt

Fully flared skirt

1 Draw a rectangle the length of the skirt × half waist measurement.

2 Divide the rectangle by folding it into four equal strips from waist to hem and cut them along the folds.

3 Spread the four pieces so that they touch at the waist and the sides, and so that the hem edges form a semicircle.

4 Draw the waist and hem curves smoothly.

Gathered skirt

1 Draw a rectangle the length of the skirt × half hip measurement plus one-third of the original hip measurement. For example:

$L \times \frac{1}{2}$ hip $+ \frac{1}{3}$ original hip

$$69 \text{ cm} \times \frac{97 \text{ cm} + 32 \text{ cm}}{2}$$

$$69 \text{ cm} \times \frac{129}{2} \text{ cm}$$

$$69 \text{ cm} \times 64.5 \text{ cm}$$

The amount added to the hip measurement may vary from as little as one-third, to three times the original hip measurement.

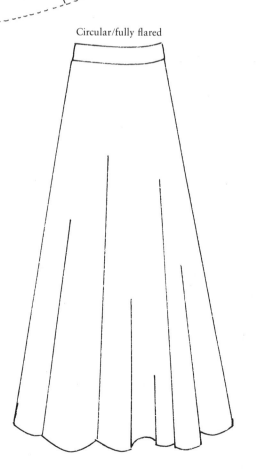

Circular/fully flared

Gathered skirt

$\frac{1}{2}$ hip + $\frac{1}{3}$

Length

C
B/C
F

Side seam

Gathered skirt with a frill

The fully shaped skirt pattern is used twice to get flare and gathers.

A section, the depth of the frill, has been taken off the bottom of the skirt and cut out one and a half times its original length.

Gathered skirt with frill

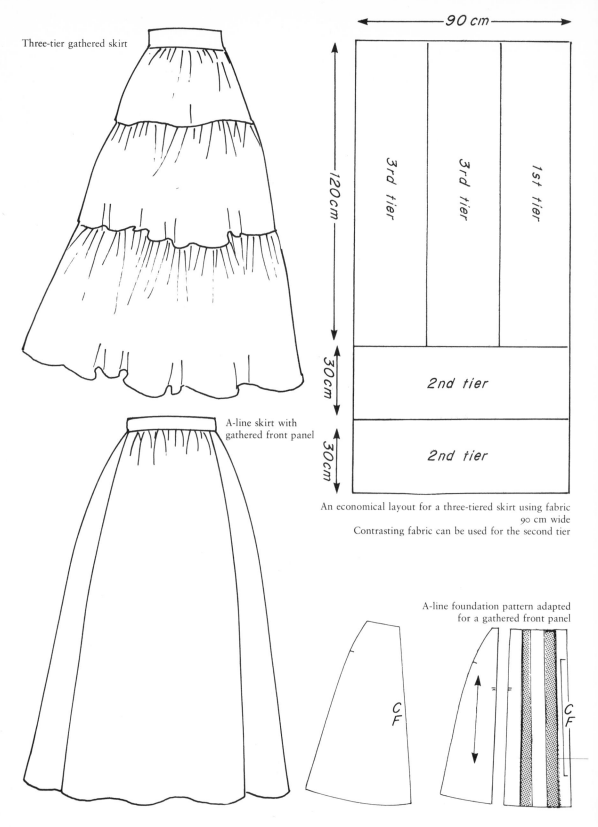

Three-tier gathered skirt

A-line skirt with
gathered front panel

90 cm

120 cm

3rd tier

3rd tier

1st tier

30 cm

2nd tier

30 cm

2nd tier

An economical layout for a three-tiered skirt using fabric
90 cm wide
Contrasting fabric can be used for the second tier

A-line foundation pattern adapted
for a gathered front panel

CF

CF

The tiered skirt

The rectangle half hip plus 4 cm × length is cut into 3 equal strips across its width. Each strip is given more fullness then the first.

The top strip can be left without any additional fullness. The second strip can be increased by half its width again. The third strip can be two, or two and a half times the original measurement. This additional fullness varies according to the weight of the fabric. A heavier fabric needs less gathers, whereas a lightweight fabric can have a great deal of fullness added. The width of the fabric being used should be taken into consideration too when deciding on the width of the tiers. Sometimes it is economical to make adjustments in the width of the tiers to fit the fabric width or when an even weave fabric is being used it may prove wiser to lay the strips along the length of the fabric.

Flared skirt with gathered panel

Either the A-line or fully shaped skirts could be used for this style with a gathered front panel.

1 Trace round the foundation pattern.

2 Cut away the section which is to be gathered. Cut and spread this to give the required amount of fullness.

The A-line and fully fitted foundation patterns cut and spread to make gathered skirts give the advantage of extra fullness round the hem with less bulk at the waist.

Pleats

The addition of fullness is an important factor in skirt designing and pleats play a large part here.

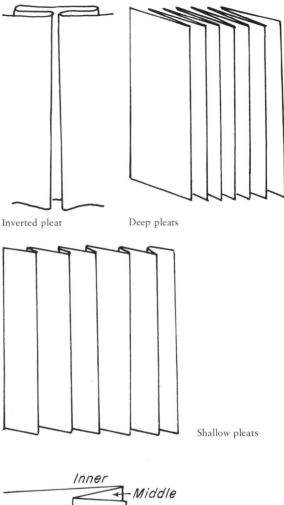

Inverted pleat   Deep pleats

Shallow pleats

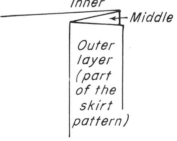

Inner ← Middle

Outer layer (part of the skirt pattern)

Knife pleats   Box pleats

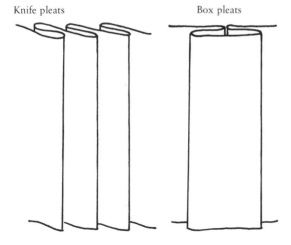

The basic pleat is a knife pleat. Two knife pleats turned outwards are known as box pleats.

Two knife pleats turned inwards are called an inverted pleat.

Pleats can be deep or shallow.

The outer layer of the pleat is part of the skirt pattern and allowance has to be made for two further layers, a middle and an inner so that a pleat is formed.

45

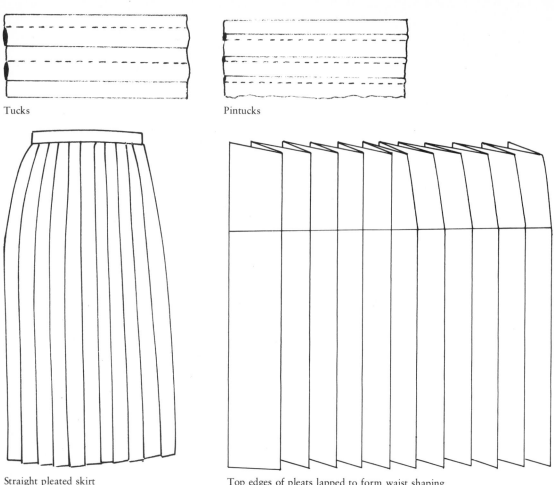

Tucks

Pintucks

Straight pleated skirt

Top edges of pleats lapped to form waist shaping

When designing skirts with pleats extra paper can be left when cutting out the foundation pattern, or spare paper and sellotape can be used.

These are the basic pleats although there are others. They may be double- or triple-layered pleats. Accordian pleats are straight pleats which overlap one another when closed and stand out like an accordian when released. Sunburst pleats are similar but are narrow at the top and wider at the bottom, producing a flare. The fabric is pleated on the bias from one corner of the length of material. These pleats are usually made by a commercial firm which specialises in this type of work. Knife pleated skirts are often made by having the fabric commercially pleated before the skirt is made up with the zip and waistband. It is advisable to make the hem before having the material pleated, leaving the side seam until afterwards.

Tucks are also a kind of decorative pleat in the form of a fold of fabric stitched.

Tucks, especially narrow ones are often made in the material before it is cut out and this will obviously not affect the pattern at all. Where tucks are part of a design, the pattern is cut and spread to accommodate them.

Pleated skirts

An all-round pleated skirt may have straight pleats which are the same width all the way down, or shaped pleats. Straight pleats are useful where a straight or very slightly shaped line is wanted or for single or groups of pleats set in below the hip line.

Straight pleats

A straight pleated skirt can be planned directly

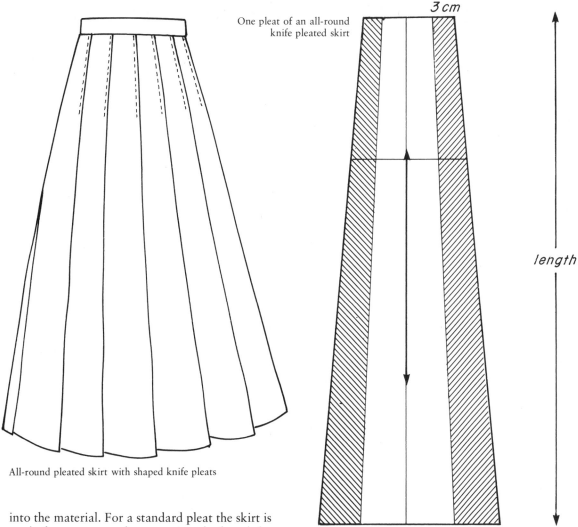

All-round pleated skirt with shaped knife pleats

One pleat of an all-round
knife pleated skirt

3 cm

length

6 cm

into the material. For a standard pleat the skirt is made from a rectangle measuring the length by three times the hip measurement, plus 4 cm ease allowance and seam and hem allowances. The material is pleated evenly either before or after the side seams are joined. The side seams should fall at the inner fold of the pleat so that they cannot be seen. The waist shaping is made by lapping the edges of the pleats at the top.

Shaped pleats

To make a skirt which is pleated all round with knife pleats where a shaped pleat is wanted, it must first of all be decided how many pleats there should be. There are two ways of making the pattern for this style. Either a pattern is made for a single pleat which can then be cut out according to the number of pleats wanted or one of the

foundation patterns can be used which would then be folded, cut and spread according to the number of pleats wanted.

A pattern for a single shaped pleat for an all-round knife pleated skirt

The waist and the hip measurement plus 4 cm must be divided by the number of pleats.

For example if 12 pleats were chosen, using standard size 14 measurements:

W 71 cm divided by 12 = 6.9 cm
H 97 cm + 4 cm = 101 cm divided by 12 cm
    = 8.4 cm

1 Draw a perpendicular line the length of the skirt.

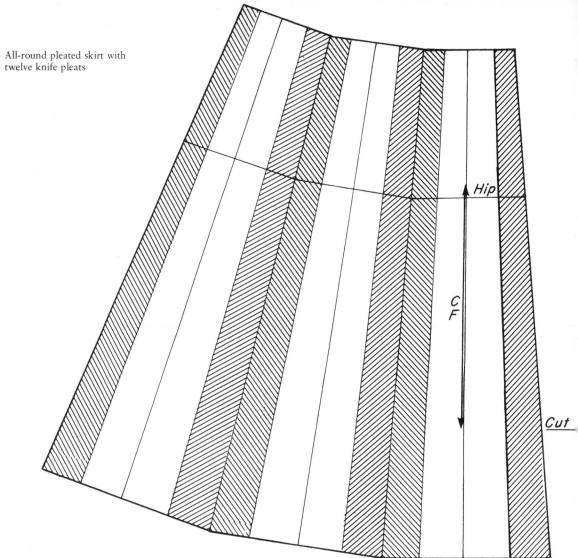

All-round pleated skirt with
twelve knife pleats

Hip

*C
F*

Cut

2 Draw a horizontal line across the top central-ised across the perpendicular. The length of this line should be the waist measurement divided by the number of pleats (in this example the length would be 6.9 cm).

3 Draw another horizontal line 20 cm down from the top line. This represents the hip line and should be centralised across the perpendicular and be the length of the hip measurement plus 4 cm divided by the number of pleats. In this example the length is 8.4 cm.

4 Draw a horizontal line along the bottom of the perpendicular about 20 cm across.

5 Draw straight lines from the top to the bottom lines making sure that these touch the ends of the line drawn across the perpendicular which repre-sents the hip.

This pattern is for the outer layer of the pleat, to which the middle and underlay must be added. The underlay may vary from a full pleat at the waist through to the hem, a narrow tuck the whole length, or a narrow tuck at the waist and a full pleat at the hem. In the example 3 cm is added at the waist and 6 cm at the hem.

Twelve separate panels can be used to make the skirt. If this method is used then as the grain would run down the centre of each pleat the skirt would hang well. As each panel would be cut out individually after added allowances for seams and hems, the result would be in effect a gored skirt.

This pattern can be used by cutting out several copies of the pleat and joining them together before laying them on the fabric. This would reduce the number of seams to be sewn up.

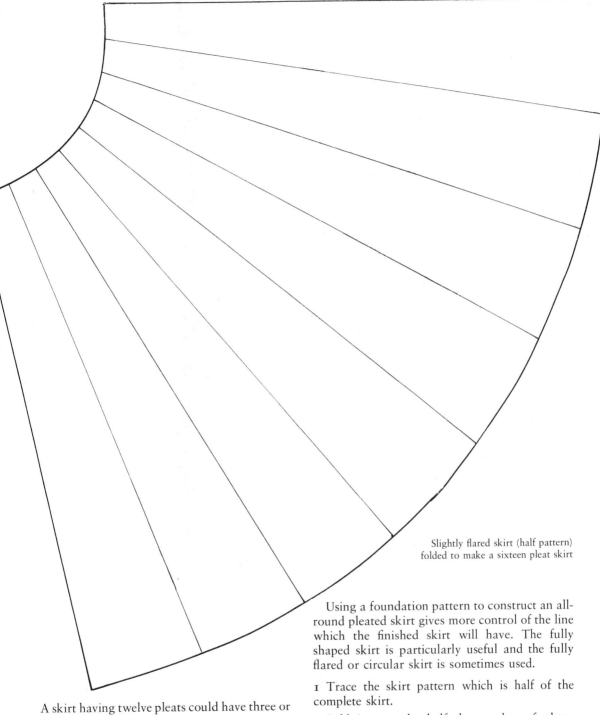

Slightly flared skirt (half pattern)
folded to make a sixteen pleat skirt

A skirt having twelve pleats could have three or six pleats joined together before cutting out, which would give a quarter or a half of the skirt. In such cases the straight grain should be directly on the CF or CB lines.

Using a foundation pattern to construct an all-round pleated skirt gives more control of the line which the finished skirt will have. The fully shaped skirt is particularly useful and the fully flared or circular skirt is sometimes used.

1 Trace the skirt pattern which is half of the complete skirt.

2 Fold it to make half the number of pleats wanted. Each of the sections then represents the outer layer of the pleat to which the underlay must be added.

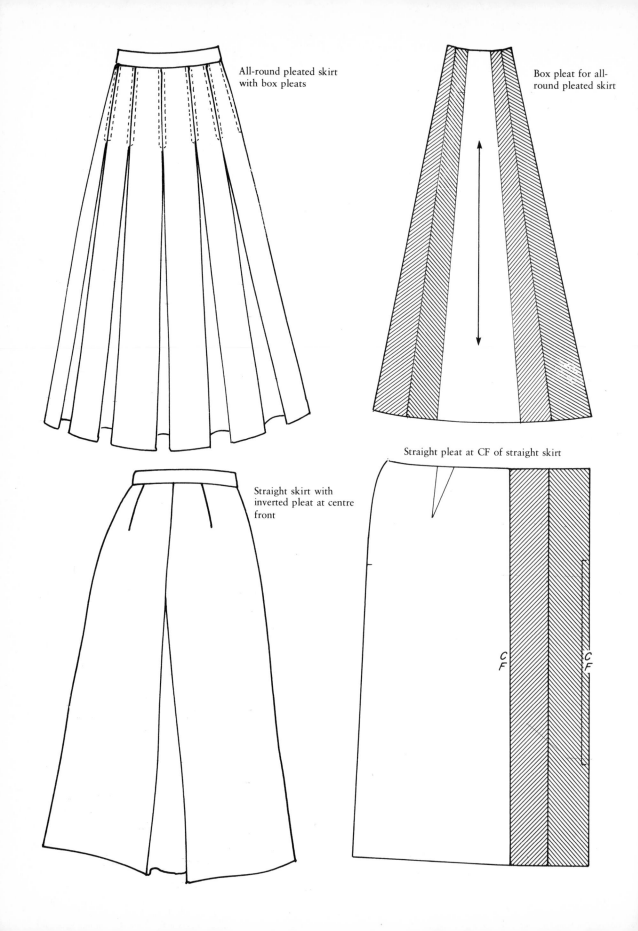

All-round pleated skirt with box pleats

Box pleat for all-round pleated skirt

Straight pleat at CF of straight skirt

Straight skirt with inverted pleat at centre front

C
F

C
F

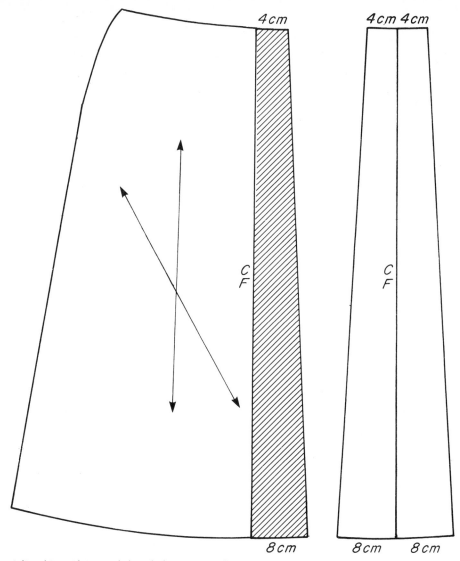

C
F

C
F

8 cm

8 cm 8 cm

A-line skirt with inverted shaped pleat at centre front

Box pleats

A box pleat has double the amount of underlay to that needed by a knife pleat.

1 Trace round the pleat panel which may have been made by either the calculation method or by folding the foundation pattern. This should not be cut out.

2 Add the depth of the pleat at the hem and the waist. In the example 2 cm have been added at the waist and 6 cm at the hem.

3 Fold under the middle layer of the pleat. Fold the middle layer back again so that the inner layer of the pleat is formed.

4 Draw along the outer fold of the pleat on to the inner layer. Cut along this line.

5 This now gives the pattern for the outer, middle and inner layers of the box pleat.

As with the knife pleat pattern this panel can be cut out singly according to the number of pleats with the grain down the centre and adding seam and hem allowances. Alternatively several pleats can be joined together before the pattern is laid on the fabric.

Pleats can also be incorporated into many styles singly or in groups. When they are included in the seams of a design, straight or shaped pleats can be used.

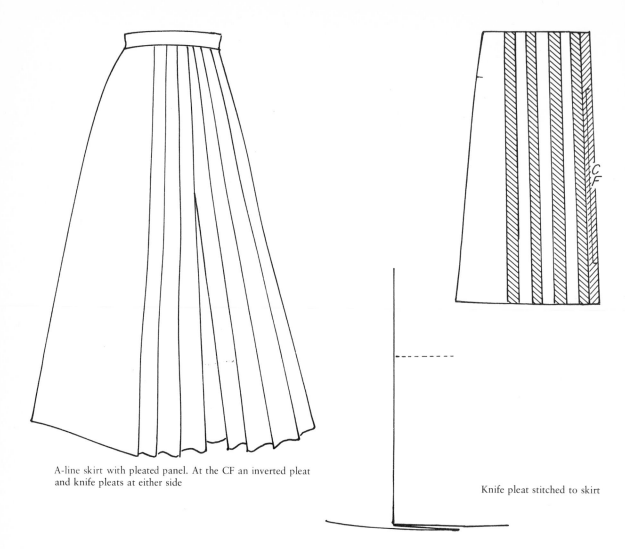

A-line skirt with pleated panel. At the CF an inverted pleat and knife pleats at either side

Knife pleat stitched to skirt

Pleated panels

1 Trace the foundation pattern which compares with the finished line of the skirt. In this example the A-line pattern was used.

2 Cut off the section which represents the pleated panel.

3 Divide the pleated panel equally into the number of pleats wanted.

4 Pin or stick the pieces on to another sheet of paper, leaving the correct amount for the middle and inner layers of the pleat.

5 Mark the CF which is to be placed to a fold.

To eliminate bulk, pleats are often cut away above the point at which they are released. They must then be supported by tape or top stitching.

Where either of these methods of supporting the pleat are not practicable, then one thickness of the pleat can be cut away, leaving the remaining thickness to support the pleat.

Pleats can be included in any part of the skirt and need not be restricted to seams, or follow a line from the top to the bottom of the skirt. Sometimes folds are used instead of pleats and the fullness does not necessarily continue through to the hem of the skirt.

Pleats are easier to crease and press if they are cut on the lengthwise grain and if the fullness is balanced. Seams are always in the inner fold of the pleat.

Pleating instructions on patterns are often shown by drawing straight lines. Circles are sometimes used.

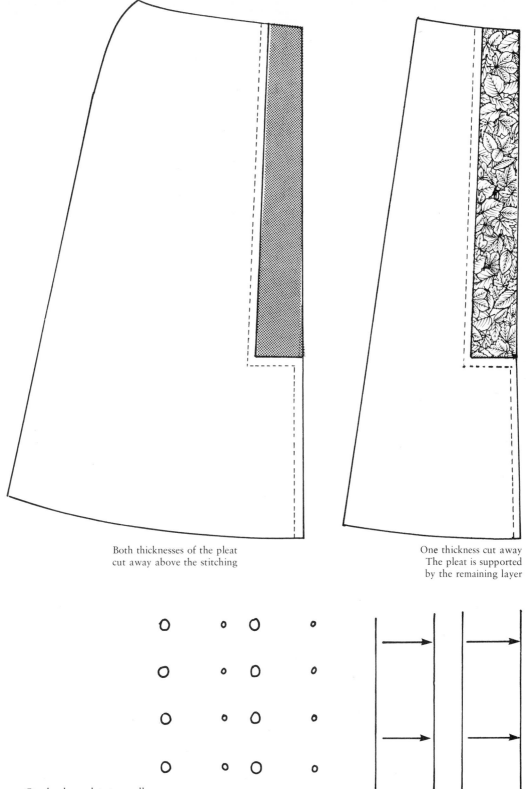

Both thicknesses of the pleat
cut away above the stitching

One thickness cut away
The pleat is supported
by the remaining layer

Overlap large dots to small

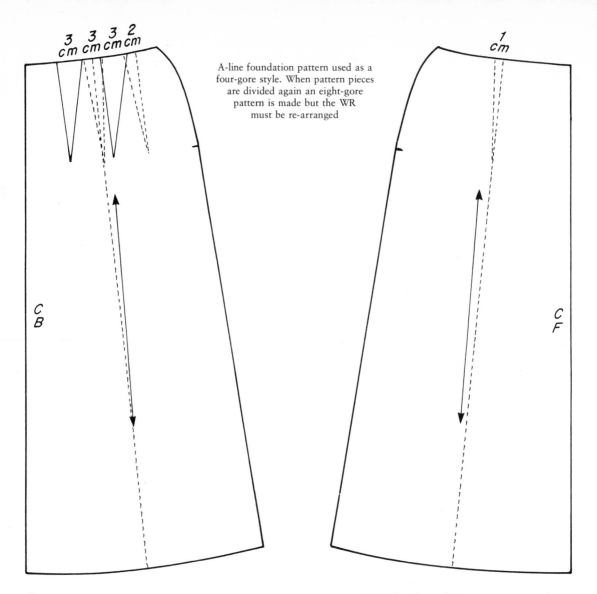

3 3 3 2
cm cm cm cm

A-line foundation pattern used as a
four-gore style. When pattern pieces
are divided again an eight-gore
pattern is made but the WR
must be re-arranged

1
cm

C
B

C
F

Gores

A gore is a section of fabric narrower at the top
than at the bottom. Any of the foundation patterns, straight, A-line, fully shaped, slightly flared
or fully flared can be divided into sections. The
more shaped the foundation pattern is, the more
shaped each gore will be. The fully shaped pattern
will have gores almost twice as wide at the hem as
at the waist.

The number of gores must be decided on and
the appropriate foundation pattern chosen. The
pattern is then divided into four, eight and perhaps
sixteen, or six and then twelve panels. They need
not necessarily be equal in width. The six-gore
skirt is particularly popular and it is often developed into more elaborate styles.

To use the fully shaped skirt pattern as a four-
gore skirt, the basic pattern is used but there will
be a seam at CF and CB instead of a fold and the
grain line will be in the centre of each panel to give
the correct hang. This method is also used to adapt
the A-line foundation pattern for use as a four-gore
style but when the A-line is divided again to make
an eight-gore, the waist reduction must be re-
arranged.

Six-gore skirt

The fully shaped skirt and other styles which have
more fullness in the hem than this are adapted into
the six-gore style by placing CF and CB to the fold
and introducing a seam between CF or CB and the
side seam.

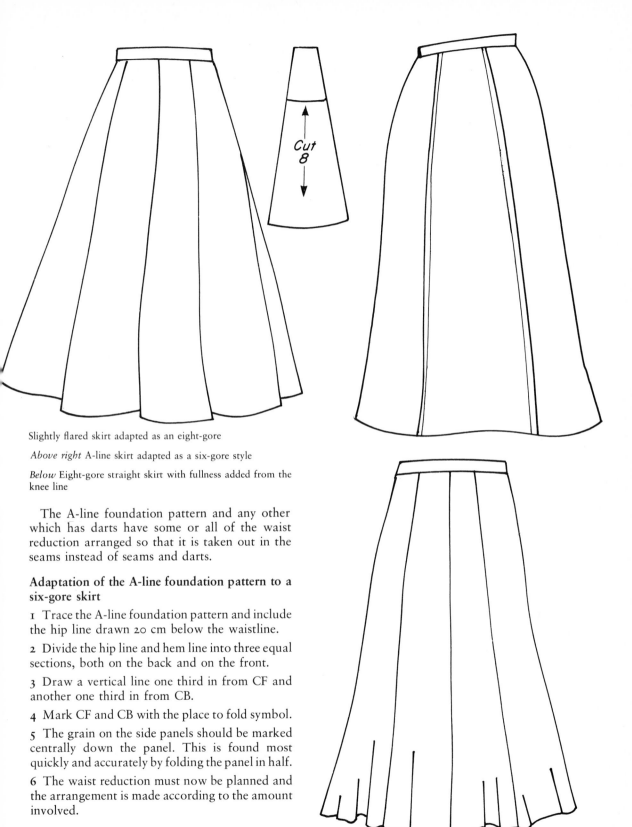

Slightly flared skirt adapted as an eight-gore

Above right A-line skirt adapted as a six-gore style

Below Eight-gore straight skirt with fullness added from the knee line

The A-line foundation pattern and any other which has darts have some or all of the waist reduction arranged so that it is taken out in the seams instead of seams and darts.

Adaptation of the A-line foundation pattern to a six-gore skirt

1 Trace the A-line foundation pattern and include the hip line drawn 20 cm below the waistline.

2 Divide the hip line and hem line into three equal sections, both on the back and on the front.

3 Draw a vertical line one third in from CF and another one third in from CB.

4 Mark CF and CB with the place to fold symbol.

5 The grain on the side panels should be marked centrally down the panel. This is found most quickly and accurately by folding the panel in half.

6 The waist reduction must now be planned and the arrangement is made according to the amount involved.

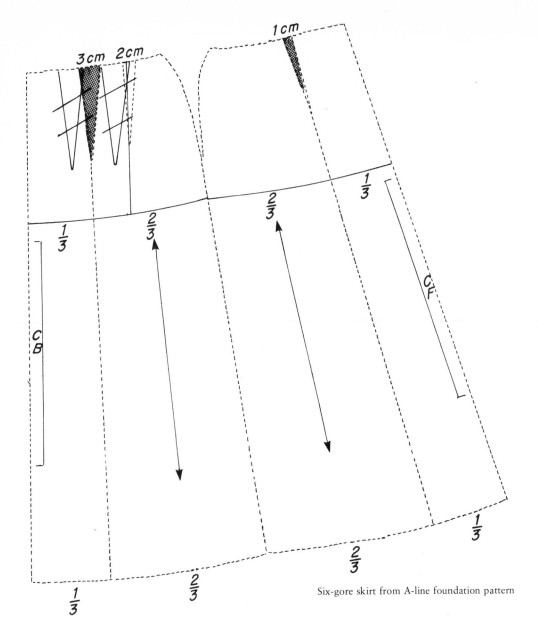

Six-gore skirt from A-line foundation pattern

Adding flare and pleats to gores

To interpret a gored style which has additional flare along the seam line there are two points to notice. Where does the fullness begin? In practice it must be drafted about 4 cm higher than it appears to develop. How full is the skirt round the hem? If a skirt is 2 metres round the hem, the hem width of the foundation pattern is deducted from the finished width and the difference divided between the gores and added as flares or godets.

Flare can be added from the yoke line, the hip line, the knee line or any point in between. The

a) 1 cm can be taken out of the side front panel/front panel, keeping the seam line of the front panel straight.
b) Up to 3 cm can be taken out of the back/side back panels.
c) Any remaining waist reduction can be taken out in a dart in the side back panel.

In the example 1 cm has been taken out of the side front/front panel, 3 cm has been taken out of the back/side panels and the remaining 2 cm has been taken out in a dart in the side back panel.

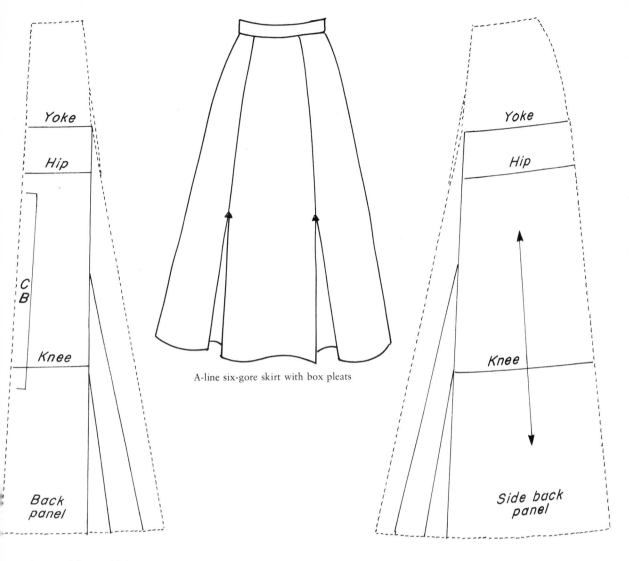

Yoke

Hip

C
B

Knee

Back
panel

A-line six-gore skirt with box pleats

Yoke

Hip

Knee

Side back
panel

Six-gore fullness added at seams

curve should be made smoothly into the original line. The amount to be added need not necessarily be divided equally between the gores.

1 Draw round the gore.

2 Decide on the additional amount to be added at the hem and the point along the length of the skirt from where the additional fullness should develop. Draw a wedge-shaped section at the side of the gore. This needs to be taken slightly higher of course than from where the fullness appears to develop.

3 The additional wedge-shaped piece should be the same length as the skirt from the point of the wedge to the hem. This will curve the hem slightly upwards.

4 Smooth the curve at the point where the extra fullness begins.

Pleats can be added to gores in the same way as they can be included in any seam, straight or shaped, throughout the whole length of the skirt or for only part of the length.

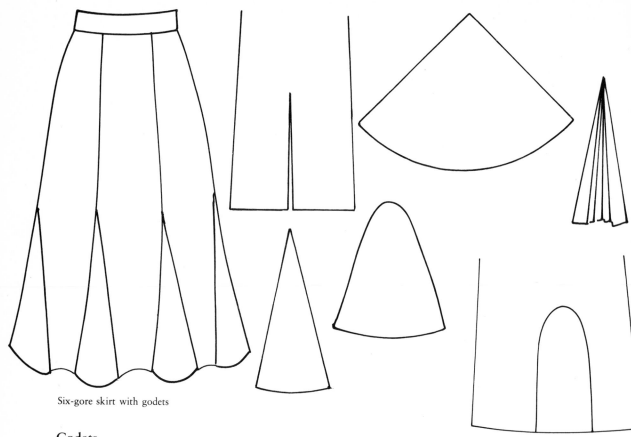

Six-gore skirt with godets

Godets

A godet is another way in which fullness may be introduced into skirts. This is basically a flared or pleated piece of fabric set-in to add width at the hem. A godet is often used in a straight skirt to give fullness from knee to hemline. Sometimes the pieces are pie-shaped, up to a semi-circle. When they are pointed or straight edged they are fitted into a seam or a straight slash in a skirt.

They may be developed from a curved or triangular section cut away from the pattern of the skirt. The piece cut away is slashed and spread to give the required amount of fullness. Very elaborate designs are sometimes developed using a godet within a godet.

Frills

Fullness can be included in a design by gathering or flaring sections of the skirt.

1 Trace round the foundation pattern.

2 Mark and cut away the sections which are to be gathered or flared.

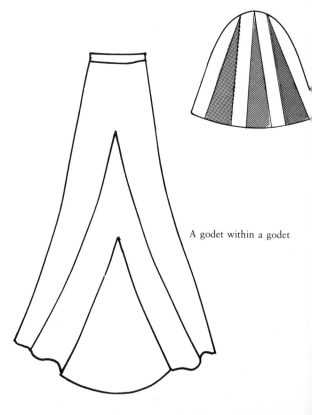

A godet within a godet

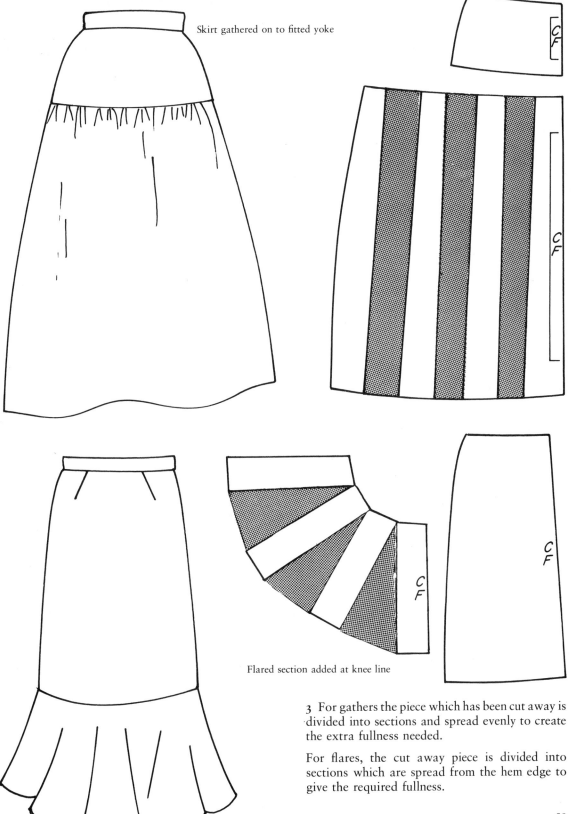

Skirt gathered on to fitted yoke

Flared section added at knee line

3 For gathers the piece which has been cut away is divided into sections and spread evenly to create the extra fullness needed.

For flares, the cut away piece is divided into sections which are spread from the hem edge to give the required fullness.

59

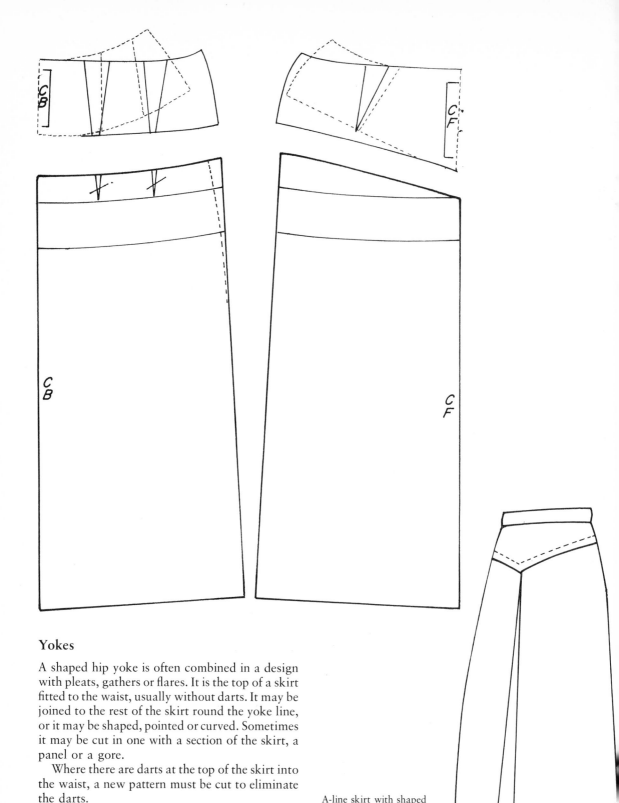

Yokes

A shaped hip yoke is often combined in a design with pleats, gathers or flares. It is the top of a skirt fitted to the waist, usually without darts. It may be joined to the rest of the skirt round the yoke line, or it may be shaped, pointed or curved. Sometimes it may be cut in one with a section of the skirt, a panel or a gore.

Where there are darts at the top of the skirt into the waist, a new pattern must be cut to eliminate the darts.

1 Trace the A-line foundation pattern.

A-line skirt with shaped yoke and inverted pleat at centre front

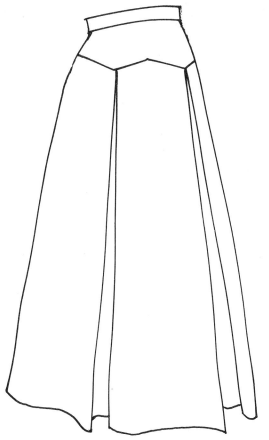

A-line with shaped yoke and inverted pleats

A-line with shaped yoke back view

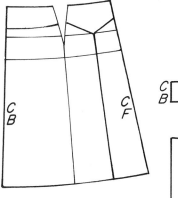

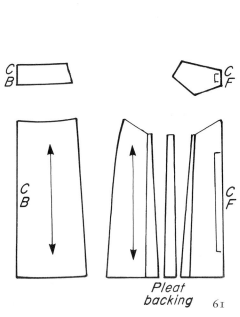

Pleat backing

2 Draw the shape of the yoke on the tracing and cut this off.

3 Re-draw the darts to the depth of the yoke and fold out.

4 Adapt the remainder of the skirt in accordance with the design.

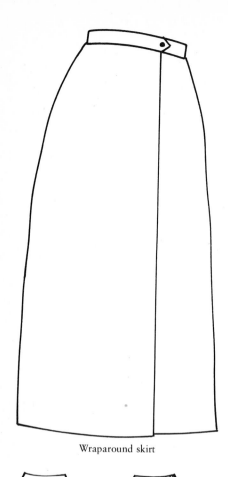

Wraparound skirt

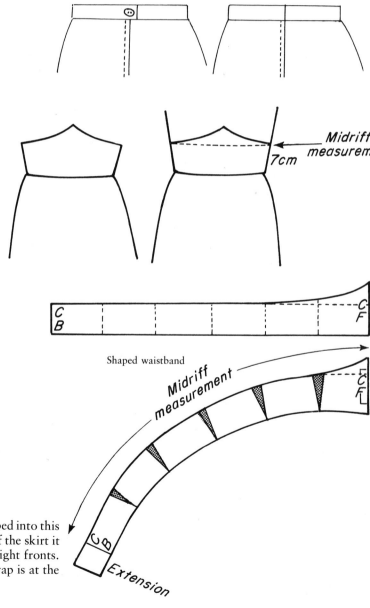

7cm

Midriff measurem

Shaped waistband

Midriff measurement

Extension

back. The under part of the wrap should go right across to the opposite side seam while the upper section is cut away at any point between the centre and the side seam.

More waistbands

The most frequently used waistband at present is a narrow band, between 2.5 and 4 cm in depth cut on the straight grain of the material. The narrow band fits the waist comfortably without any shaping. Wider bands need shaping to fit the curve of the waist.

Left front   *Right front*

Wraparound skirts

Any foundation pattern can be developed into this style. If the wrap occurs at the front of the skirt it will have differently shaped left and right fronts. The opposite will be the case if the wrap is at the

1 Draw a rectangle half waist measurement × depth of waistband.

2 Cut and spread the upper edge of the waistband until it compares with the midriff measurement at the top of the waistband.

3 Add an allowance for the extension on either the left back or right back.

Where a waistband is fastened with buttons the extension is allowed on the left and right to allow the button to sit on the centre or seam line. Where concealed fastenings are used, the extension is just made on the right, to give a neat finish to the waistband when it is fastened.

For a waistline finished with a shaped facing the top of the skirt is traced off for the depth of the facing. After closing the darts the facing piece is cut either in one or two sections. This facing is sometimes more elaborately shaped and fitted to the outside of the skirt, possibly with the dart fullness in the lower skirt being incorporated as a soft pleat.

Waistline finished with decorative facing similar to a narrow yoke

Pockets

Patch pockets may be simple or elaborate with tabs, pleats, tucks, topstitching, binding and cuffs. They are sewn to the outside of the skirt and vary in size from very small to enormous and may be decorated with a flap at the upper edge. There is a great deal of scope for imaginative ideas in designing and placing patch pockets.

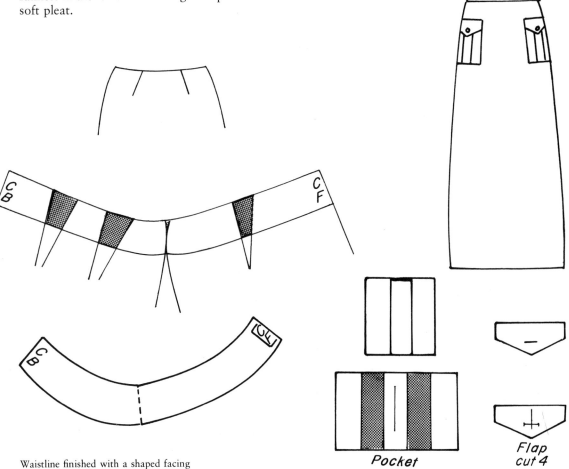

Waistline finished with a shaped facing

Pocket

Flap
cut 4

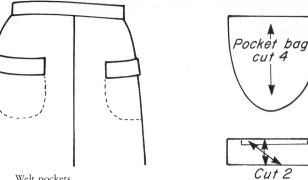

Flap pockets

Welt pockets

Pocket bag cut 4

Cut 2
Flap/welt

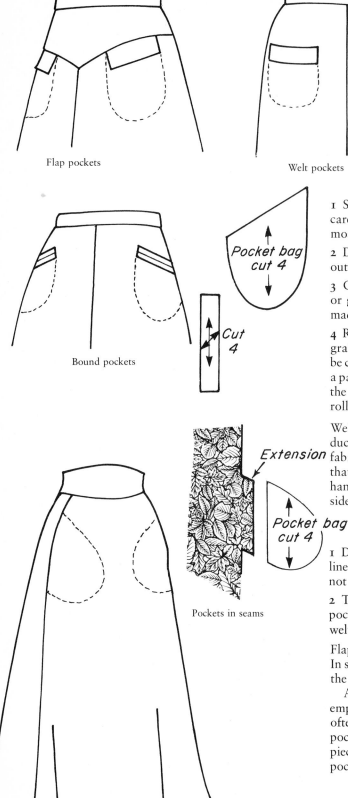

Bound pockets

Pocket bag cut 4

Cut 4

Extension

Pocket bag cut 4

Pockets in seams

1 Sketch the pocket on the skirt design after carefully considering the size of the pocket and the most suitable place for it.

2 Draw the pocket as a paper shape using the outer dimensions of the pocket.

3 Cut the paper and open it out to allow for pleats or gathers in the same way that adaptations are made to skirt patterns.

4 Re-cut the pattern adding facings. Mark the grain and indicate how many of each section must be cut out in fabric. Where a heavy material is used a patch pocket is often lined to reduce bulkiness. If the lining is cut slightly smaller the seam line will roll into the inside.

Welt and bound pockets are sometimes introduced into a seam or may be fitted into a slit in the fabric. Welt and flap pockets are similar except that the flap pocket is usually loose and the flap hangs down whereas the welt is stitched at the sides.

1 Draw the pocket on the skirt pattern. Use dotted lines to show those parts of the pocket which will not be seen.

2 Trace the pattern pieces for the sections of the pocket, under pocket, upper pocket, bindings, welts or flaps.

Flaps and welts are occasionally purely decorative. In such cases there is of course no need for a slit in the garment or the construction of a pocket bag.

A pocket in a seam may be concealed or emphasised with topstitching. Part of the pocket is often made of lining to reduce bulk. Sometimes a pocket in a seam is cut in with the main pattern pieces, but it is often more economical to cut the pocket bag separately.

1 Decide on the position and shape of the pocket and draw this on to the skirt pattern.

2 Add an extension to the skirt at the pocket opening.

3 Trace the shape of the pocket bag.

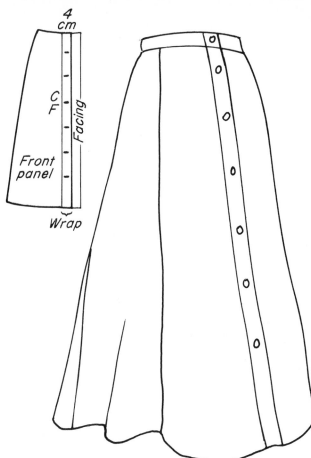

Slightly flared skirt with eight panels and buttoned fastening at CF

Hip pockets

Where part of the skirt is cut away to reveal the under pocket, two differently shaped pieces are needed for the pocket bag.

Buttoned openings

Skirts which are fastened with buttons all the way or part of the way must have an extension to allow for the wrap. This is often about 4 cm. At other times it is planned according to the width of the button to be used.

When the skirt is buttoned there should be half a button's width between the edge of the button and the finished edge of the skirt. A large button may have an extra centimetre added to this.

65

Technique

Hand stitches

Before the invention of the sewing machine in 1755, it is difficult to believe that some of the beautiful costumes worn by our ancestors and displayed in their portraits, were all made completely by hand. In spite of our devotion to the sewing machine there is still room for hand stitches to play a part in skirt making.

Running stitch Running stitches are similar to tacking, but are worked as small as they can be comfortably sewn. To begin, two or three stitches are taken on the spot and the thread is pulled tight. A thimble is useful as it protects the middle finger when taking up three or four stitches on the needle at one time. To finish off, two or three stitches are again worked on the spot.

Back stitch This is a strong stitch which looks like machining on the right side. The needle goes back to the last stitch before being taken forward to make the next stitch.

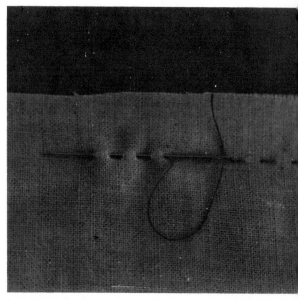

Running stitch
Back stitch

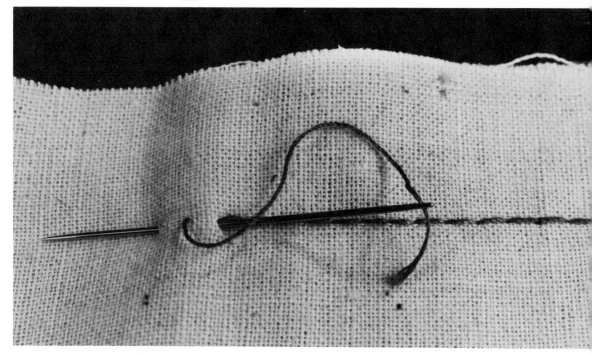

Occasional back stitch Strength is added to running stitch by making a back stitch at intervals.

Prick stitch Similar to back stitch but the needle is only taken over one or two threads of fabric before moving on across the underneath to the next stitch. This stitch is used for decoration as well as for putting zips in by hand.

Slip stitch This stitch is used where the stitching should not be seen, particularly for hems. The needle is slipped through the fold of one side and then two or three threads are caught on the other side. The stitches should be no more than 5 mm long.

Hem stitch On the wrong side hemming stitches show as a slanting stitch. They should not show at all on the right side.

Above right Occasional back stitch

Right Prick stitch

Below right Slip stitch

Below Hem stitch

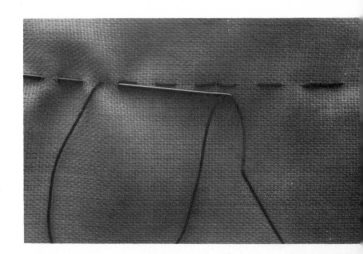

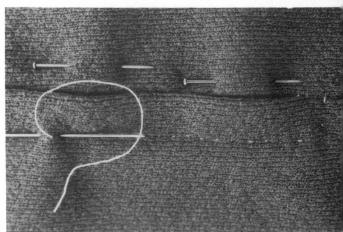

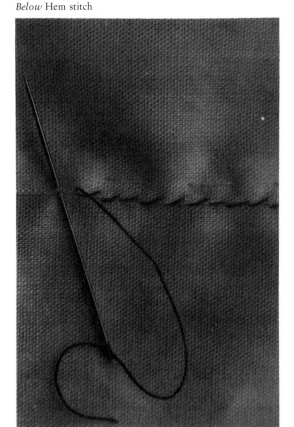

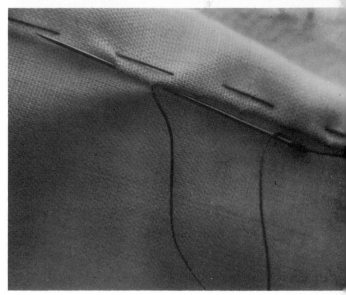

Lapped seam

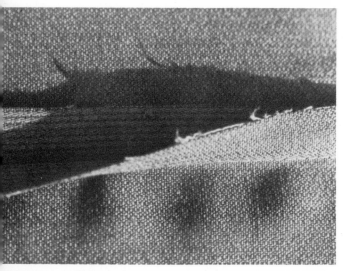
Plain seam

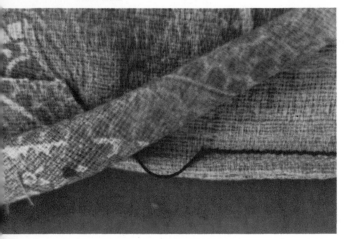
French seam

Pinning and tacking seams

After some practice most people can machine straight seams without pinning or tacking. This is not practicable where one of the edges is longer and must be eased against the other to make it fit, for example a skirt on to a waistband, or where the edges are curved. Such seams must be held together by pins and tacking stitches before being put to the machine.

Seams to be joined should be placed together with raw edges level and the pins put into the fabric at right angles to the seam. Pin at each end, matching edges and then the layers in the area in between are evened out. Where seams cross they must match.

Pins placed at right angles to the direction in which the machine needle is travelling do not need to be taken out as the seam is stitched since the machine needle will slide over the pins. Some fabrics tend to bunch at the pins and it may be necessary to take the pins out while the seam is being stitched.

Of course the seam should be stitched along the seam line or fitting line, which is usually 1.5 cm from the edge of the fabric. Seams should be stitched in the direction of the fabric grain to help prevent stretching and reduce fraying.

Seams

Plain seam This seam is the one most commonly used for joining two sections of fabric together. The pieces to be joined are pinned right sides together and machined or hand stitched along the seam line. The seam is pressed open and if the fabric frays, the edges must be neatened.

Lapped seam A useful seam for attaching yokes. One piece has the seam allowance turned under and pressed. This is then lapped over the other section and top stitched.

French seam The pieces to be joined are placed wrong sides together and a plain seam is hand sewn or machined 1 cm from the edge. It should then be trimmed to about 3 mm and pressed open. After turning the fabric right sides together the seam is pressed flat. Another row of stitching along the seam line which can be between 4 mm to 1.5 cm from the edge, completely covers the raw edges of the first seam. This seam is often used for sheer fabrics when it is worked as narrow as the fabric will allow.

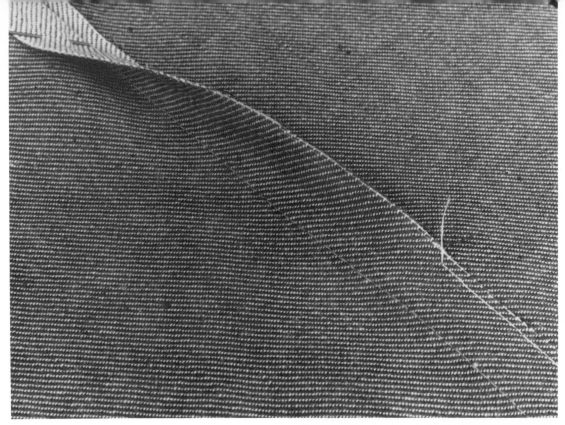

Welt seam

Machine felled seam

Welt The welt seam is similar to the machine-felled seam on the right side but it is used for bulky fabrics which fray very little or not at all. A plain seam is stitched. The seam allowances are pressed open and then to one side. The underneath seam allowance is trimmed to 4 mm. The upper seam allowance is pressed over the trimmed edge and stitched close to its raw edge.

Machine felled For sportswear where a strong seam is needed a machine felled seam is ideal. The pieces to be joined are placed wrong sides together and a plain seam is stitched. The seam allowances are pressed to one side and the lower seam allowance is trimmed to 4 mm. The other seam allowance is pressed over the trimmed seam with the raw edge turned under. The seam is stitched again through all thicknesses along the folded edge. The seam is not suitable for bulky fabrics.

Fastening off

Fastening off machining can be done by hand or by machine. By hand the ends may be brought to the same side and tied in a knot. Alternatively, one end can be threaded into a needle and a double back stitch worked, taking in the last stitch of the machining. This is useful for darts in unlined garments where a neat strong finish is wanted. Skilful machinists will be able to reverse the machine so that several stitches are sewn over the last few stitches of the seam. This needs care as the

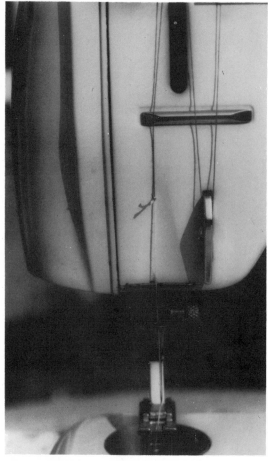

Fastening off avoided by machining a dart with a continuous thread

Overcast edges

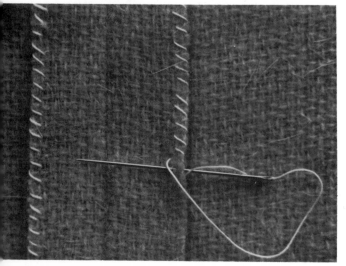

reversed stitches must lie directly over the stitches of the seam they are finishing off. For the less experienced it might be considered safer to leave the needle in the fabric at the end of the seam, raise the presser foot and turn the fabric right round, stitching several stitches in a forward direction along the seam to be finished.

The problem of finishing threads at the end of the dart can be avoided altogether and this is very useful when working with sheer fabrics. Thread the top of the machine in the usual way but the needle should not be threaded, except to bring the thread up from the spool in the bottom of the machine. The machine needle should be threaded with the thread from the bottom of the machine. The thread from the top of the machine should be joined to the thread from the bottom of the machine with a knot. The reel of thread on the top of the machine should then be wound up, taking in as much thread as will be necessary to machine the dart without the knot appearing. The dart is then machined in the normal way but there will be no ends to finish off.

Staystitching Edges which may stretch before the garment is sewn together, either because they are bias cut or the fabric is stretchy, need to be staystitched. Staystitching is a row of machine stitching through a single thickness of the fabric close to the seamline. Matching thread is used and normal stitch length.

Dealing with fraying edges

Edges which are enclosed in a facing, a seam or a lining which is fixed are not usually neatened. Where edges fray and are open to friction in wear and washing they must be protected.

Zigzag machining This should be worked on the edge. The depth and width of the stitch depends on the fabric. A smaller stitch is used on closely woven fabrics and a wider one on loosely woven fabrics.

Overcast edges Small even stitches are made over the raw edge. They should not be pulled tight. A row of machining, using a long stitch, is sometimes made along the edge to act as a guide to keep the overcast stitches even.

Blanket stitch This stitch is worked on the edge. It is often used to supplement other forms of neatening perhaps where a zip has been fitted or to fix the bottom of the zip tapes to an opening.

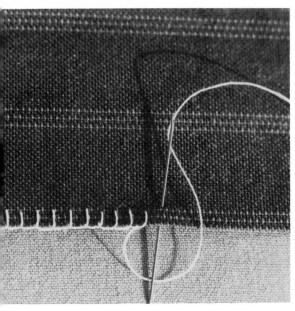

Blanket stitch

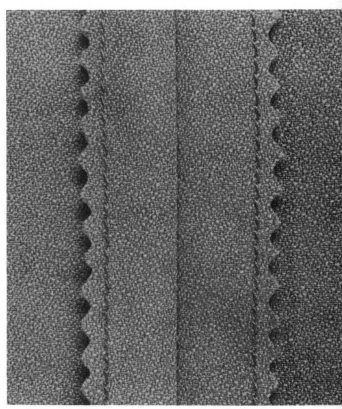

Machined and pinked edges
Binding

Machined and pinked Where the fabric frays only slightly the edges can be machined using a straight stitch about 4 mm from the edge. The raw edge is then trimmed with pinking shears.

Turned and stitched The raw edge of the seam is turned under 5 mm and then machined 3 mm from the fold. This method is most useful for medium and lightweight fabrics which are firmly woven, such as cotton. It is not suitable for bulky fabrics.

Binding The raw edges can be bound with straight or bias seam binding depending on whether the seam is straight or curved. The binding can be applied in two steps by machining one side of the binding to the edge and hemming the other edge to the machine stitches.

Alternatively, it can be folded and pressed so that the under section is 2 mm wider than the upper section. Commercial bias binding is often similarly stepped. The binding is slipped over the raw edge and tacked and machined close to the edge. Having the deeper layer underneath will ensure that both edges are caught in the machining.

Trimming, clipping and grading

Seams are trimmed to reduce bulk. Where there are several layers of fabric in a seam allowance they should be trimmed at different widths to

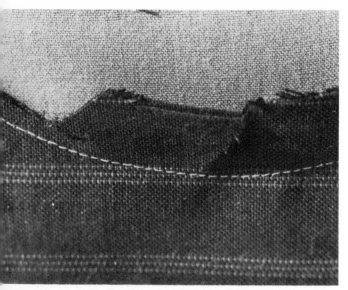

Seam allowances clipped on an inward curve

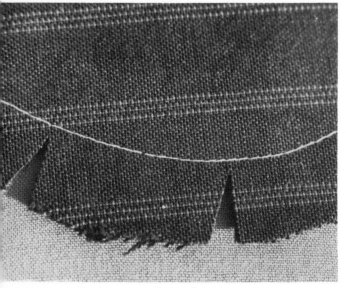

Notches cut out of seam allowances on an outward curve

Interfacing

Interfacings are either woven or non-woven. The woven interfacings may be made of cotton, wool, goat hair, rayon, polyester or a mixture of any of these. Non-woven interfacings do not have grain and so pattern pieces can be laid in any direction. It is machine washable and does not fray. It varies in thickness and the fleece weight can be used for padding and warmth. It is available in white, black, grey or natural. Some are stretchable and others stable. Stretchable interfacings must be handled like a woven fabric because there is stretch in the crosswise grain but none in the lengthwise grain.

Both the woven and non-woven are available either to be sewn in, or fusible. Fusible interfacing is coated with a resin which melts under the heat of an iron to fuse it to the garment. It should be tested on a scrap of fabric to make sure it does not show through. Many fusibles need steam or a damp pressing cloth. Pressing should be carried out with an up and down and not a gliding action.

Fusible web has resin on both sides and can be used at hemlines to fuse two pieces of fabric together. Another specialised development is useful for giving a permanent crease to pleats. The interfacing which is fusible is manufactured in strips with slits along the centre. This is pressed to the wrong side of the skirt with the centre of the interfacing strip against the fold of the pleat.

Interfacing gives stability to the fabric, adds body and crispness. It should never be heavier than the fabric. If the interfacing is draped over a chair with the fabric on top, the interfacing should not impose its fold through the fabric. More than one kind of interfacing may well be used in one garment, when consideration is given to the waistband, the yoke, the pockets, the pleats and the hem.

Pressing

Careful pressing is essential at every stage. Creases should be removed before cutting out, fabrics may have to be pre-shrunk and each seam should be pressed as it is stitched and certainly before it is crossed with another seam.

In addition to an iron, an ironing board and a sleeve board are essential. Closely woven cheese-cloth or muslin makes an excellent press cloth because the steam can penetrate the loose weave and yet the threads keep the iron off the surface of the fabric.

prevent a ridge forming. This is called grading seam allowances. The widest seam allowance is next to the outside fabric.

Curved seam allowances should be clipped so that the seam can lie flat. On an inward or concave curve the seam allowance is trimmed or graded and clipped to the stitching line with snips about 1 cm apart. On outward curves after grading the seams, notches are cut to the line of stitching about 1 cm apart.

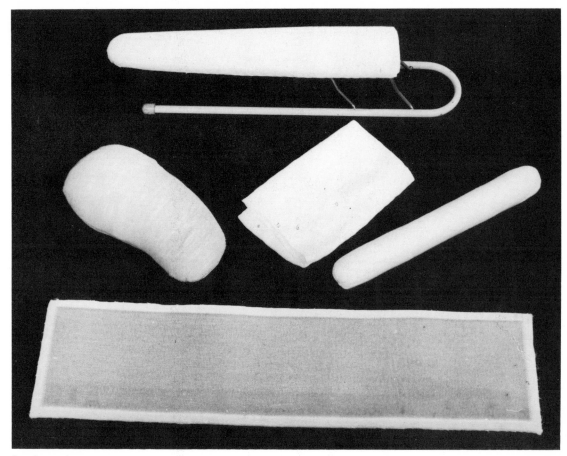

Pressing equipment

A tailor's ham is a ham-shaped cushion used for pressing curved or shaped areas. This can be made by cutting two oval pieces of fabric about 20 cm by 30 cm. Firmly woven cotton can be used on one side and fine wool or flannel on the other to make the ham more versatile. The oval is sewn round the edges, turned, stuffed hard with kapok or polyester stuffing and the opening sewn up.

A seam roll is a large firm sausage which is useful for pressing seams open where the fabric is delicate and an impression of the edges of the seam allowance would be pressed through to the right side of the fabric when the seams are being pressed open. A seam roll can be made from a wooden rolling pin wrapped in two or three layers of flannelette. The final layer should be stitched smoothly in place.

A needleboard is an expensive piece of equipment but, of course, once acquired it will prove very useful for velveteen, velvet and other pile fabrics, preventing them from matting and marking by allowing the pile to fit between the needles as the seams are pressed open.

Pressing is carried out with an up and down movement rather than a sliding movement which is associated with ironing. The fabric should be pressed with the grain line, parallel to the selvage rather than diagonally across the fabric which could stretch it and pull it out of shape. On crease-resistant fabrics especially, the fold line from the roll might prove difficult to remove even with a damp cloth and a hot iron and the only solution is to avoid that area when cutting out the skirt.

Cotton and linen Press with a high temperature on the wrong side. No press cloth needed. Moisture might be needed to make seams sharp. Watch for shine particularly on dark colours when a press cloth would be needed.

Wool Moderate heat and a damp press cloth. Press as much as possible on the wrong side.

73

Silk Moderate heat on wrong side, possibly with a dry press cloth.

Man-made fibres Low temperature on wrong side. Too much pressing of white fabric can cause yellowing.

The question of correct pressing is, however, made much more complex by the fact that fabrics are made up of mixtures of fibres and because there is such a wide range of weaves and knits.

Difficulties caused by varying fibre content

The fabric and thread must be compatible. Pressing a cotton fabric which has been sewn with synthetic thread might result in the hot iron needed for the cotton damaging the sewing thread.

Fabrics sometimes shine after pressing. A damp press cloth and hot iron might prevent this, but if not, a dry wool press cloth between the damp one and the fabric might help. If the shine persists a hot or medium hot iron used with a dry cloth on the wrong side of the fabric may prove satisfactory. Fabrics with an acrylic or polyester content often come into this category.

On very springy fabric it is sometimes difficult to get a sharp crease with the limited weight of domestic irons. This can sometimes be overcome by laying the seam open along the ironing board and spongeing along the seamline, followed by pressing with a damp cloth. The extra steam may give the crisp effect wanted.

Some man-made fabrics become permanently marked if they are pressed with a hot iron as the fibres to some extent dissolve with the heat and cannot be restored, so caution is needed.

Water should never be allowed to come into contact with silk and some taffeta fabrics as they may become permanently marked.

There are many possibilities and variations. The safest advice is to check on a piece of the fabric the best way to press to get a good finish.

Where there are difficulties, experiment in this order:

1 Dry cool iron on wrong side and right side.

2 Dry medium/hot iron on wrong side and right side.

3 Medium/hot iron with damp press cloth.

4 Medium/hot iron with damp press cloth and dry wool cloth between.

5 Medium/hot iron with dry press cloth.

6 Medium/hot iron with dry press cloth of similar fibre content to fabric, ie silk on silk, wool on wool.

Difficulties caused by fabric construction

Crêpes and other fabrics with raised surfaces may need very careful pressing with a cool iron on the wrong side to prevent the surface being damaged. Fabrics with a pile weave such as mohair and velvet need special care too. Sometimes these fabrics can be pressed with a hot iron and although this may mark the pile, if it is brushed before the fabric has cooled and dried after pressing, the pile may be restored and the seam lie sharp and flat. The needleboard is the best way to press these fabrics but where this is not available and the fabric marks badly, the iron should be stood on its heel and the back of the seam to be pressed held against the hotplate of the iron.

Seams

Seams should be pressed along the stitching line before being pressed open. Flat pieces should be laid on the ironing board but where shaping has been introduced into the fabric with darts or seams, this must not be shrunk out or wrinkled by pressing the area on a flat surface. It must be allowed to take up the built-in shape over a sleeve board or tailor's ham. Seam imprints can be avoided by using the seam roll. In the case of hems, tucks or pleats, strips of a fairly strong paper, such as brown wrapping paper, can be slipped under while pressing to prevent impressions being made on the right side. Where seams are to be pressed to one side they should be pressed open first to avoid any unwanted tucks appearing on the right side.

Darts

Darts should be pressed on both sides along the line of stitching, using the tip of the iron. Brown paper may be needed here too to prevent a ridge appearing on the right side. Darts in bulky fabrics should be trimmed to 2 cm from the point and pressed open. The final part of the dart will be pressed in the shape of a triangle. Vertical darts are usually pressed towards the centre back or centre front.

Pleats

Pleats should be pressed lengthwise along the pleat folds while they are still tacked, first on the right side and then on the wrong side. The pleats should not be pressed to the hemline until after the hem has been turned up. After turning up the hem the whole area of the pleats should be pressed again. A damp cloth might be needed to remove marks made by tacking threads.

Check beforehand to see that marks left by tacking threads can be removed. If there is any difficulty then the pleats should be pressed and the tacking stitches taken out before the fabric has cooled. The pleats should be pressed again immediately.

Gathers

The iron should never be placed flat on top of a row of gathering as the effect would be spoilt by the large number of creases which would be made. The gathered edge should be lifted and the gathers pressed with the point of the iron.

Zips

Press zips over a tailor's ham to retain the curve of the hip seam. A hot iron should not be allowed to come into contact with a nylon zip as it might be damaged.

Hems

Hems should be pressed before they are finally sewn. After the hemline has been marked the skirt

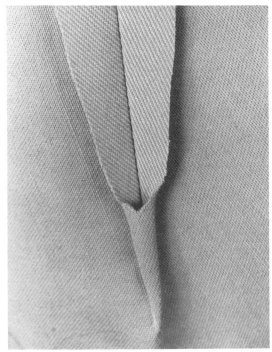

Dart trimmed and pressed open

Hem pressed with paper between the layers to protect the right side

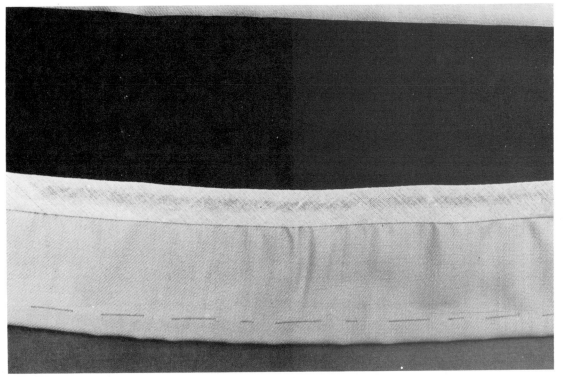

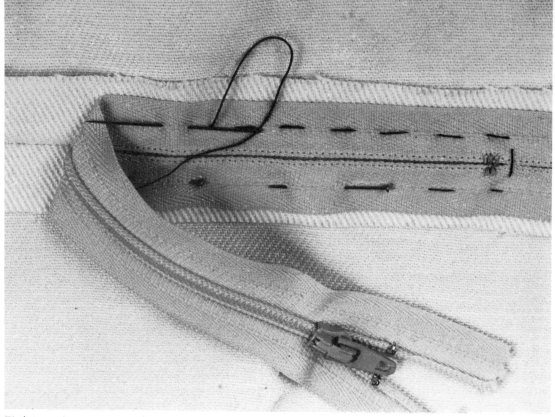

Zip being tacked to wrong side for a slot seam application

should be laid wrong side up on the ironing board. The fold of the hem should be pressed with a piece of paper between the hem allowance and the skirt.

A soft pad or folded towel laid over the ironing board prevents impressions being made on the right side from zips or the inner construction of bound buttonholes.

Zips

Zips for skirts are usually between 15 and 23 cm long. Where the skirt is slim fitting the minimum opening for comfort is 18 cm. Zips may have metal teeth or synthetic coil and may be invisible or regular.

Zip fasteners should be fitted as early as possible in the making-up process as it is much easier to fit the zip when both sides of the opening lie flat. Certainly the zip must be fitted before the waistband is attached. The opening may have to be adjusted slightly to fit the length of the zip which should have the fabric slightly eased on to it to make sure that it lies absolutely flat. Stretch fabrics need stay-tape tacked to the wrong side along the seamline before the zip is applied. For any success-

ful zip application, the seam allowance must be a minimum of 1.5 cm.

A zipper foot is very useful as it allows the machine to stitch close to the teeth without the foot sliding about.

Machining past the slider without causing the stitching line to swerve is difficult. The best way is to leave the machine needle in the fabric, raise the foot and move the slider out of the way, if necessary removing tacking stitches from the seam, while stitching that particular section of the seam.

Regular zips are usually fitted into a lapped or a slot seam.

Either method can be carried out by hand using a prick stitch.

For slot seam

Tack together the opening in which the zip is to be fitted, either by hand or by machine. The seam allowance should be pressed open and flat. The closed zip is tacked to the skirt centring the zip teeth over the seam line. On the outside the zip is stitched 6 cm either side of the seam line. The bottom of the zip is sewn either with square or arrow-shaped corners.

Underlapped edge folded in a further 3 mm for a more concealed zip

The edge of the opening close to the zip can be hemmed in place with small stitches

Although this is an easy method it sometimes proves difficult on smooth, light-coloured fabrics to machine accurately enough to get the two sides of the seam absolutely equal.

For a lapped seam

It is still a good idea to tack the opening by hand or machine to begin. Press the seam open and take out the tacking stitches. This gives a good straight edge on which to work. To make the zip more concealed than in the simplest method described on page 24, the seam on the underlapped edge should be folded a further 3 mm in from the fitting line, making a small fold in the seam allowance at the bottom of the zip opening. The zip can then be machined in with the underlapped edge close to the teeth and the lapped edge machined 1 cm away from the fitting line.

Another variation on sewing a zip into a lapped seam is to hem the narrow edge of the opening to the edge of the zip teeth. This method is invaluable if there is no zipper foot available, and for pile fabrics.

Where it has been found difficult to machine the lapped seam in a straight line, this row of machining 1 cm from the edge can be sewn before the zip is put in. The zip can then be tacked to the back of the lap just inside the machined line. Finally the zip is hemmed to the back of the machining with small stitches.

To strengthen the end of the opening and to give the bottom stop added support at least one row of stitching should be sewn across the bottom of the zip or a bar tack should be worked.

The invisible zip is suitable for most fabrics. The finished effect shows no stitching and the seam continues in an uninterrupted line. The invisible zip is sewn to the opening edges before the rest of the seam is stitched. For the successful application of an invisible zip, it is best to buy the special sewing machine foot, sold where the invisible zips are sold, and follow the maker's instructions.

Zip shield

To make a shield to lie at the back of the zip.

1 Cut a piece of material on the straight grain the length of the zip tapes and about 9 cm wide. Fold the fabric double lengthwise and press. A piece of broad grosgrain ribbon could be used instead of the fabric.

Zip stitched close to the edge of the zip shield

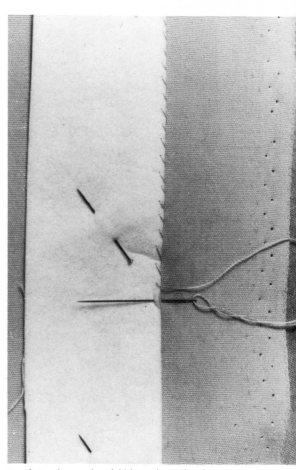

Interfacing hemmed to fold line of waistband

2 Stitch the zip to the right-hand side of the shield close to the edge.

3 The zip is then sewn into the skirt in any of the ways already explained except that the other edge of the tape must be sewn to the skirt without the stitches going through the shield. The sewing across the bottom of the zip must go through the shield, as well as the skirt and the zip tapes.

Waistline finishes

A waistband is the most usual waistline finish. The skirt at the upper edge should be about 2 cm larger than the waistband and this fullness eased on to the band to allow for the hip curve. The waistband is usually cut on the straight grain. To eliminate bulk the selvage is sometimes used for the inside of the waistband so that it will not be necessary to turn the inside edge under.

Zip sewn to the left hand side of the skirt opening in the normal way

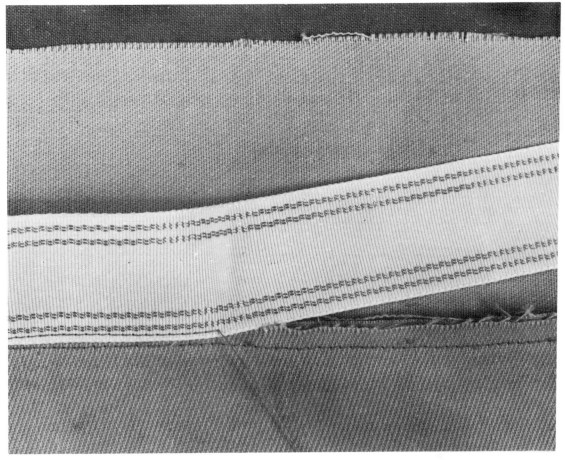

Waistband stiffening machined to the seam allowances above the waistline

It is very important that a waistband does not crumple or roll. Interfacing is sometimes used to give body and prevent stretching. The interfacing should be cut half the width of the waistband pattern and tacked to the inside of the edge of the waistband. It is then hemmed to the fold line. Iron-on or fusible interfacing is also cut to half the depth of the waistband with the side which is ironed-on placed to the inside. Petersham which may be boned, or stiffening materials produced especially for waistbands in various widths, are useful. If the stiffening is quite firm or iron-on there is no need to slip stitch it at the fold of the waistband.

Belt interfacing can be used in the waistband. After the waistband has been attached to the skirt right sides together, the stiffening is machined to the seam allowance of the waistband before the waistband is turned over and attached to the back of the skirt.

Grosgrain ribbon can be used as a backing to the waistband instead of a double layer of material being used. The outer layer of the waistband should have the seam allowance tacked over the interfacing. It can then be topstitched, the lower edge of the topstitching fastening the waistband to the skirt. The grosgrain ribbon is hemmed to the back of the waistband. Alternatively the grosgrain ribbon may be machined to the front waistband before it is attached to the skirt.

The waistband can be topstitched in place by sewing it first of all to the wrong side. The waistband is then folded over to the right side and topstitched close to the edge of the waistband. This topstitching can be continued round the waistband.

A deep waistband will need a very firm interfacing to keep it smooth and if it is shaped at the waist it might stretch. To prevent this a strip of straight

79

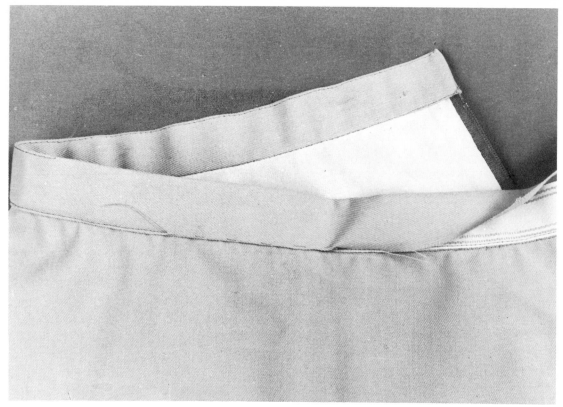

Waistband topstitched in place on the right side

seam binding should be incorporated in the waistline seam.

Where a skirt has no visible waistband it can be finished either with grosgrain ribbon or a facing.

The facing will be the same shape as the top of the skirt and should be attached to the skirt right sides together, incorporating straight seam binding into the seam to prevent stretching. After stitching, trimming and grading the seams, the facing should be understitched to keep it in place. The lower edge of the facing should be neatened by overcasting or zigzagging, avoiding any methods requiring a turning which might show as a ridge on the right side. This loose edge should be sewn to the zipper tape, any darts and the seams. A hook and eye will be needed at the top of the closing.

If grosgrain ribbon is used a 2.5 cm strip should be cut to fit the waist measurement with 2.5 cm extra. The grosgrain ribbon can be machined under the seam allowance at the waistline, in which case the seam will have to be neatened, or it can be laid over the waistline seam and topstitched close to the edge.

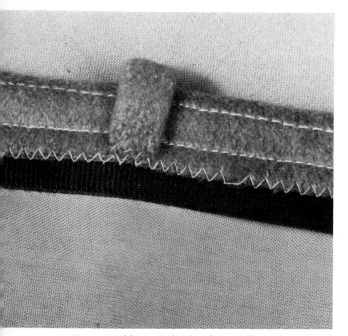

Grosgrain ribbon waistband with seam allowance machined over it

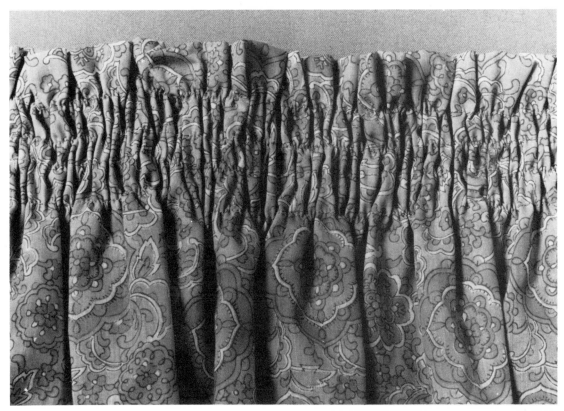

Elasticated waistline using shirring elastic

Waistlines of lightweight fabric may be elasticated with several rows of shirring elastic. This narrow thread-like elastic is wound round the spool of the sewing machine by hand. The top tension may need releasing slightly before a good stitch is obtained.

On stretch fabrics particularly elastic is used at the waistline. The elastic can be sewn directly to the edge of the skirt at the waistline or it may be slotted through a casing. The elastic should be cut up to 5 cm shorter than the waistline measurement and joined with a 2 cm seam, strengthening it by opening it out and stitching diagonally from corner to corner. The elastic is then stitched to the edge of the waistline along the seamline on either the right side or the wrong side depending on whether or not the elastic is to be hidden under the fabric. Straight or zigzag stitch can be used. A second row of stitches is needed to hold the other edge of the elastic in place. Where elastic is to be slotted through a casing the latter must be as wide as the elastic with about 5 mm to spare, plus seam allowances. It should be as long as the area round which it is to be fitted, plus seam allowances. More

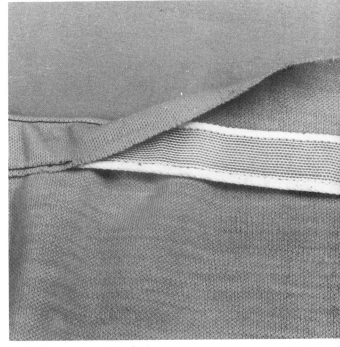

Broad elastic as a waistline finish

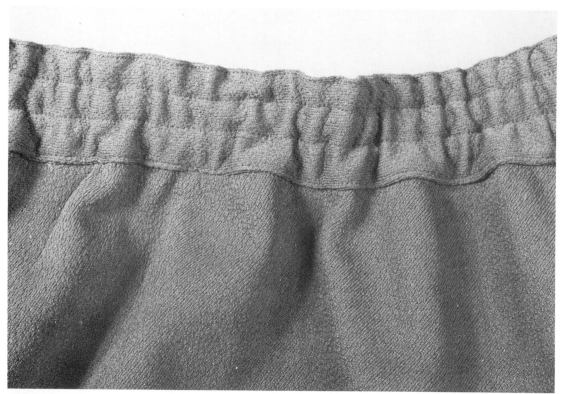

Belt carrier

Above left 1 cm wide elastic slotted through channels
Below left Drawstring waist finish

than one layer of elastic is sometimes used in which case slots are needed to keep the elastic separated.

Drawstrings are sometimes used in place of elastic in a casing with possibly the addition of top stitching at the upper edge to give a frilled effect.

Belt carriers

Belt carriers are used to hold belts in place at the waistline. They can be made of fabric or thread.

Fabric loops are made by cutting pieces of the fabric twice the finished width plus seam allowances. After machining, the seam allowances should be trimmed before the loops are turned right side out. They are made in various widths from 4 mm to 5 cm and may be arranged singly half way between centre back and side seams and centre front and side seams or just at the side seams and centre back. Sometimes they are arranged in groups of two or three. They can be plaited or crossed for a more decorative effect.

The loops can be incorporated into the waistband seams or carried over the top and stitched to the back of the waistband. They can be turned in at the ends and stitched on top of the waistband. A wide belt carrier might be used to support a narrow belt and in this case the belt carriers must be top stitched to give a narrow slot.

Belt carriers are usually made from straight strips of fabric cut on the straight grain. If the selvage is used the loop is folded in three with the selvage on top. This is then hemmed down. For plaited belt carriers rouleau strips would have to be used.

Belt carriers made of thread are usually designed to be unnoticed. They are made of a row of blanket stitches sewn closely together over a foundation of three or four strands of buttonhole twist slightly longer than the width of the belt.

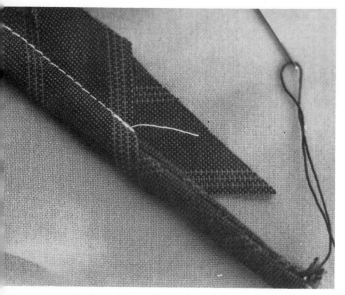

Rouleau strip/trimmed and turned

The hook is sewn to the overlap of the closing edges about 3 mm away with either buttonhole or overhand stitches. The stitches should not of course show on the right side. The eye or bar is sewn to correspond on the opposite side of the opening. The thread eyes are made of matching thread when blanket stitches are worked over three or four strands of thread.

For sportswear particularly the hammer-type press-on snap fasteners which can be applied with a special pressing tool are available with an attractive variety of decorative heads.

Nylon closure tape is a useful additional aid to neat skirt fastening. Although it is not fine enough to use in place of the zip it is useful for the inside edge of a wraparound skirt as well as waistbands. It should be machined to the waistband before it is folded over so that it is fastened very firmly and no stitches show on the right side.

Buttonholes

The most usual buttonhole on a waistband is either hand sewn or machined. The machined buttonhole should be made in accordance with the instructions given with each individual make of sewing machine. Hand sewn buttonholes are easier to work if the correct thread which is buttonhole twist and a fine needle are used. Buttonholes should never be worked through only one thickness of material as this will not support the stitching. They should be worked through the top of the fabric, interfacing and the facing section.

It should be remembered that when the buttonhole is horizontal the button sits at the end of the buttonhole, not in the middle, and the buttonhole must be at least 3 mm longer than the button. Buttonholes should always be made along the straight grain of the fabric otherwise they will stretch out of shape or have a wavy line.

After making the buttonhole and cutting along the line, the edges of the buttonhole should be overcast with matching thread to hold the three layers together.

Horizontal buttonholes are made with fan shaped stitches at the edge where the button sits and a bar at the inner end to prevent stretching. The buttonhole stitches are started at the inner end, worked down one side of the opening, around the point with the stitches spread like a fan and then down the other side of the cut. The stitches are worked from right to left and kept close together. At the inner end several stitches are made

Hammer type snap fasteners with fixing tools

Fastenings

Hooks and eyes or bars are made in a wide range of sizes and give a secure fastening often used in conjunction with press-studs. They consist of a hook and either a bar which is used when the edges of the closing overlap, or a round eye which is used when the edges just meet. In either case they may be replaced with a thread bar which gives a particularly inconspicuous closing above a zipper.

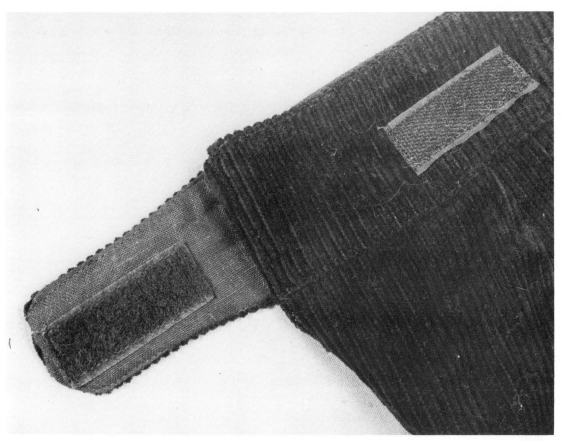

Nylon closure tape

across the slit for the bar tack. Blanket stitches are worked over these threads and through the fabric.

There are several methods of making bound buttonholes but, because of the limited area in which to work they are not usual on a waistband. They may be necessary for a skirt which has buttons and buttonholes in the main area of the skirt, perhaps all the way down the front, or from yoke to hem.

The buttonhole can be marked on the wrong side of the fabric which will have interfacing attached. It can be marked with a fine felt tip pen or a pencil. A patch about 6 cm deep and 2.5 cm wider than the buttonhole should be centred over the buttonhole on the right side and tacked in place. Working on the wrong side, the buttonhole is stitched 3 mm above the marked line, directly across the end, 3 mm below the marked line and directly across the other end. After machining the buttonhole is cut along the marked line and into the corners to within a thread or two of the machining. The patch is then pulled to the inside, drawing it back

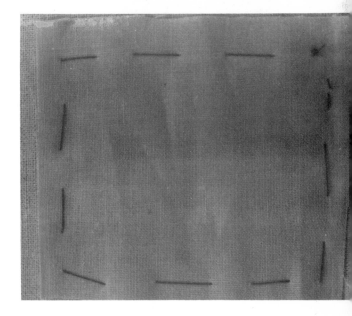

Patch tacked to right side of fabric

85

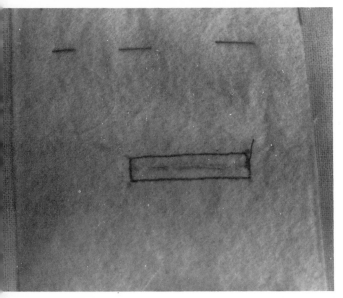

Buttonhole machined on wrong side

Patch pushed through to the wrong side, forming tucks across the hole

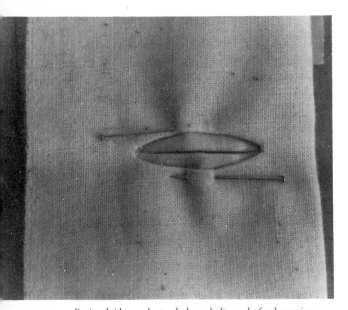

Facing laid over buttonhole and slit ready for hemming

at the corners and allowing two tucks to form across the buttonhole opening. The tucks are stitched on the wrong side to keep them in place. The final stage is to fold the facing over the buttonhole and cut a corresponding slit which should be turned in and hemmed with small stitches at the back of the buttonhole.

Buttons are either the sew-through type or have a shank, which is an extension from the button either of metal, cloth or the same material as the button. They should be sewn with a heavy duty thread or regular thread drawn through a block of beeswax, used double. The shank of the button is to allow for the thickness of the fabric at the buttonhole. If the material is very bulky then the buttonhole will need a deeper shank. Possibly even where the button has a self shank, additional allowance will have to be made for the thickness of the material.

Two or three stitches are made on the right side where the button is to be sewn. The needle is brought through the button and back into the fabric, a matchstick or something similar can be laid over the button under the first stitch to allow for a thread shank. The sewing is continued until enough stitches have been made and the matchstick can be taken out. The button is given a pull to even out the stitches and the thread wound tightly round the stitches under the button to make a shank. The sewing is fastened off with two or three stitches on the spot.

Hems

The fabric used and the style of the skirt determine the depth and type of hem used. Flared skirts, bulky or knit fabrics should have narrower hems. Straight skirts or lightweight fabrics can have a wider hem. Sheer fabrics may have a very narrow rolled hem or a wide hem depending on the cut. A skirt with a bias or circular hem should hang overnight to allow the bias to drop before the skirt is levelled.

To level the hem the skirt should be worn with appropriate shoes and the body weight evenly distributed. The hemline should be marked an even distance from the floor. A pin or chalk marker is a great help, or a friend with a metre stick and pins.

The hem of long skirts often proves difficult to mark. This can be made easier by marking a distance of say 15 cm from the ground which gives a level line and then with the skirt laid flat on the table another line can be marked which indicates the required amount off the ground, which will be a fixed distance from the line already marked.

Where the seam allowances of the skirt extend into the hem these should be trimmed to reduce bulk. Where seams have been neatened together as they would be in pleats, the seam allowance must be opened out and trimmed within the hem.

The hem should be folded along the pin or chalk line and tacked 5 mm up from the fold line. It might be necessary to even out this line made by the pins or chalk as the hem must look straight and fold up smoothly even if it means it is slightly uneven. The effect of plaids and checks must be considered carefully, each case individually, so that the finished effect looks right.

The depth of the hem allowance having been decided, the actual hem allowance must be levelled too, with the help of a piece of card in which a notch has been cut to indicate the width of the required hem depth. There might be quite a lot of fullness in the hem of a flared skirt which must be shrunk or gathered out before the hem is sewn up. A row of machine stitches 3 mm from the raw edge using a long stitch which will gather should be made. The gathering thread is drawn up so that the raw edge lies flat against the skirt. A piece of paper is slipped between the hem and the skirt and the raw edge is pressed with a damp cloth. This will either shrink out the excess material or compact the gathers making them easier to handle. Bias binding is sewn on to the raw edge of the hem and then slip stitched to the skirt. If the fullness is only slight it can often be eased on the stitching line.

If bias binding is not used, the raw edge of the hem allowance must be dealt with in accordance with the fabric and the style. Where the raw edge is

Seam allowance trimmed within the hem to reduce bulk

zigzagged, machined and overcast, or machined and pinked, then the hem is blind stitched. Where the hem is turned under twice or finished with bias binding, slip stitch is used.

A soft hemline is sometimes wanted and this softness is often achieved with interfacing. Bias strips of woven interfacing are cut the same width as the hem allowance and long enough to round the hem. The raw edge of the hem must be finished off. The interfacing is tacked to the wrong side of the hem, extending it 1.5 cm below the hemline. The top of the interfacing should be blind stitched to the skirt or herringboned to the underlining if one has been attached. At the hemline the interfacing is caught to the skirt with long and short running stitches. The hem is turned up and attached with blind or slip stitch. It should then be steamed, not pressed. If the skirt fabric is suitable this effect can be achieved by using iron-on interfacing.

A hand rolled hem is often used for sheer fabrics. A row of machine stitches is made along the hemline or slightly below and trimmed close. The edge is then rolled very finely between thumb and forefinger and stitched invisibly. Where the fabric does not fray a narrow machined hem can be used. A row of machining is made along the hemline which is then folded up and edge stitched 3 mm or so up. The raw edge is then trimmed to the second row of stitching.

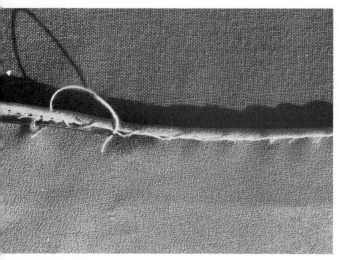

Hand rolled hem

Skirts made from knitted fabrics should also be hung before being hemmed. Apart from the traditional hemming methods a lettuce or ripple hem is sometimes sewn. The hem allowance is trimmed to 1 cm and turned to the wrong side. The folded edge is stitched using a medium zigzag stitch. The hem edge can be deliberately stretched while it is being sewn to increase the ripple effect.

Where a fairly deep hem is used on a heavy fabric two rows of blind stitching will prevent any sagging occurring. One row is worked half way up from the hemline and the raw edge and the other close to the raw edge.

Lightweight fabrics look attractive with a top stitched hem. Three or four rows of machining spaced up to 6 mm apart can be worked using silk buttonhole twist and a longer than usual stitch length.

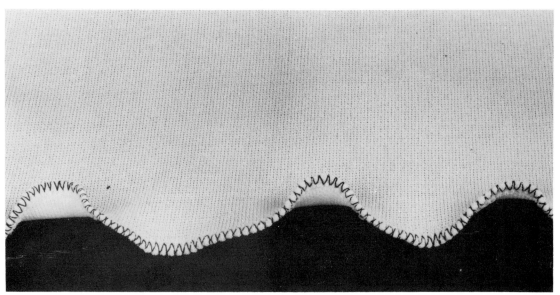

Lettuce hem

Specialised cutting and handling

Cutting out bias and circular skirts

Where a skirt is bias cut, or consists of a full circle, it may be necessary to piece the material. The width of the fabric determines the need for piecing. Where a fabric is more than 170 cm wide, piecing will not often be necessary, but where the skirt pattern pieces are wider than the fabric, new seams must be made. Some bias cut full-length skirts cannot be cut in one piece even with the widest fabric.

1 Pin the pattern on the fabric, matching grain lines.

2 Allow the extra pattern to project and cut it off 1.5 cm in from the edge of the fabric. Draw the grain line on this piece parallel to the original grain line.

3 Use this piece of the pattern now by laying it on the fabric, again matching the grain.

4 Cut the extra piece out with seam allowance on the edge which is to be joined.

5 Join the extra piece to the main part of the skirt before beginning to put the skirt together.

Striped fabric

Stripes may be even or uneven. When using striped fabric, styles with seaming interest are to be avoided. The fabric must create the design.

Crosswise stripes These are matched across the centre front, centre back, and side seams. A dominant stripe should be avoided at the hip line, but if possible should run along the fold of the hem.

To cut out striped fabric it should be folded so that the stripes are matched perfectly at the selvages, and pinned to avoid any danger of their slipping out of position.

For uneven stripes, a with nap layout should be used, ie, all the pieces must lie in the same direction.

Lengthwise stripes If a seam line is straight the stripe will match evenly lengthwise. If the seam-line is not on the straight grain the stripe will

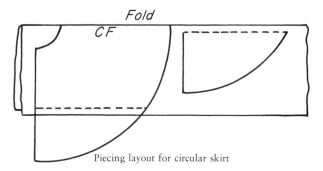

Fold

CF

Piecing layout for circular skirt

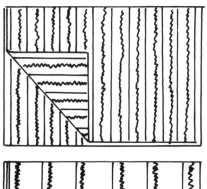

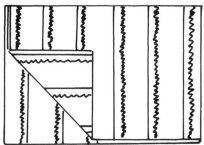

Even or balanced stripes   Uneven or unbalanced stripes

create a V-shaped effect called a chevron. The more biased the seamline, the more defined the chevron will become. The chevron is sometimes a planned design feature. The grain line for a four-gore skirt with a chevron design at the centre front must be adjusted so that it has a bias grain line which is at an angle of 45 degrees from the original. On seamlines, stripes are matched by relating corresponding notch marks on the pattern. To make sure that the chevron matches perfectly, the seams must be slip tacked before machining.

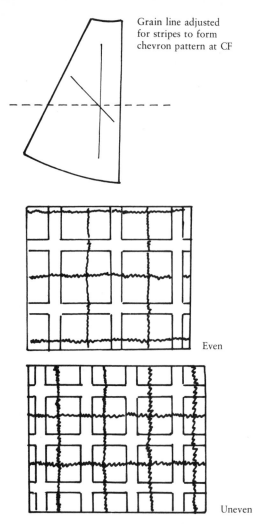

Grain line adjusted for stripes to form chevron pattern at CF

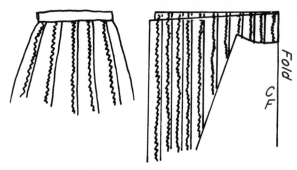

An uneven stripe forming a continuous pattern round a skirt

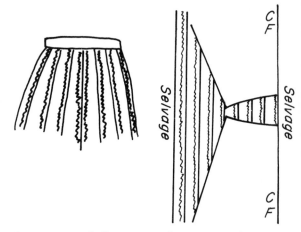

For a symmetrical effect or mirrored image reverse the pieces and cut on a single fabric

Even

Uneven

Other fabrics have the same characteristics as stripes in that there is a pattern which runs throughout the length or width of the fabric. It may even be diagonal. In these circumstances, the fabric must be treated as striped when planning the cutting layout and making up.

If there is a yoke, avoid matching the stripes, as the yoke may be camouflaged out of existence. Stripes moving in a different direction may be much more effective.

When the fabric is fairly firmly woven it is often possible to use horizontal stripes as vertical stripes, by placing the pattern pieces on the crosswise grain, rather than the lengthwise grain.

If, despite careful planning, the stripes will not match up at the seams, concentrate on the centre front and centre back seams, and ignore the side seams.

An uneven or unbalanced vertical stripe can form a continuous repeat pattern round the skirt. By using a centre front and a centre back seam a symmetrical effect is created.

Plaids

Plaids are designs where there are stripes crossing each other at right angles. Plaids can be even, or uneven. Designs which are to be made up in plaid fabric should be kept simple, with a minimum of seam lines, and detail restricted to flaps, welts or patch pockets with the plaid cut on a different grain.

When cutting out, the dominant lines should be used for finding the straight grain. The most attractive place for the dominant lines must be settled. This could be on the centre front and

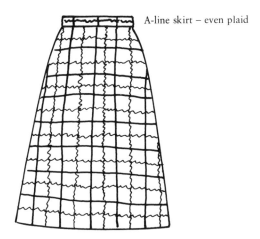

A-line skirt – even plaid

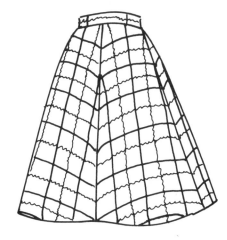

Chevrons formed at CF, CB and side seams in an even plaid

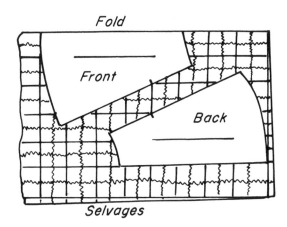

Fold

Front

Back

Selvages

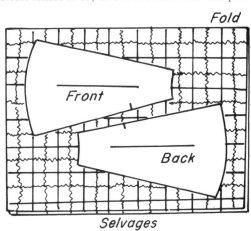

Fold

Front

Back

Selvages

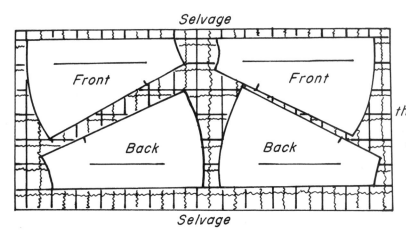

Selvage

Front   Front

Back   Back

Selvage

Single
thickness
of
fabric

Right Uneven plaid – design arranged in opposite directions from CF

91

centre back, or equidistant from these.

Uneven plaids, like uneven stripes, can be made to go round the body in one direction. Alternatively, they can go in opposite directions from the centre front and centre back. For this symmetrical, or mirrored effect, the pattern pieces must be cut singly, then reversed and turned upside down before they are cut singly again. After cutting out one pattern piece the lines of the plaid can be copied on to the edge of the paper pattern which will make placing the pieces on the fabric again and matching up the plaid lines much easier.

Diagonal stripes

A design with the minimum of pattern pieces should be chosen and, of course, darts should be avoided if at all possible. A *with nap* cutting plan will be necessary and it will be easier to work on a single thickness of fabric.

Knitted fabrics

Knitted fabrics vary considerably in weight, texture, fibre content and stretchability. If they are fairly firm they have many of the properties of woven fabrics and can then be tailored, and yet have a soft look. They are probably best unlined, but if a lining is wanted it would be better if a fabric with some stretch, such as tricot, were chosen. Care should be taken not to stretch the fabric as it is being machined, with either a stretch stitch, a zigzag stitch, or two rows of machining very close together.

The more stretchable knits can be shaped rather than darted, but as there is a wide range in the degree of stretch and return to original size, care is needed. To check the recovery of the fabric hold a folded piece of fabric and pull it in the direction of the selvages until it reaches the maximum extended width. If, when it is released, it returns almost to its original size, it will not become shapeless during construction or wear. If the recovery is poor the garment could be underlined, but this is often unsatisfactory and generally the best solution is to use a gathered style which would avoid the fabric being stretched during wear.

Before making up, seams which must retain their shape should be stay stitched. A row of machining is made through a single thickness of fabric, normal stitch length, just inside the seam allowance. A man-made or combination

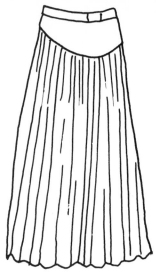

Single jersey.
Yoke interfaced and lined, suitable for soft jersey with poor return

polyester/cotton thread will be necessary if the sewing machine is straight stitch only, but if the machine will do a stretch, or zigzag stitch, the thread can be chosen to match the fibre content of the fabric. Ballpoint needles push the threads of the fabric aside, rather than breaking through them and sometimes causing runs.

Fusible interfacing, particularly the non-woven kind that stretches only in the crosswise direction is useful for knitted fabric. Fusible webs disappear when used in hems or facings and will not prevent the knit from stretching, but of course they always need testing first in case any problems might arise.

To prevent later shrinkage it may be necessary to pre-wash knits and this too may help to remove the fold along the length of the fabric. It is wise to check that this can be removed so that if it cannot, it can at least be avoided when cutting. *With nap* layouts are often necessary as shading can show up in a finished garment, particularly when using raschels which are usually bulky or textured.

Some seams may need to give with the fabric, while others need to be kept firm. For stretchy seams a narrow zigzag stitch, or the stretch stitch of the sewing machine, can be used. To prevent seams from stretching a narrow straight seam binding, or twill tape, should be machined in with the seam. If seam neatening is necessary, zigzag, or edge stitching without turning is useful.

Sheer fabrics

These can be soft like georgette and chiffon, firm like voile, or crisp like organdy and lace.

Cutting-out can prove difficult. A felt surface, or

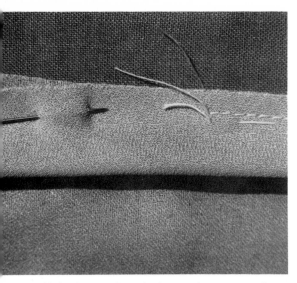

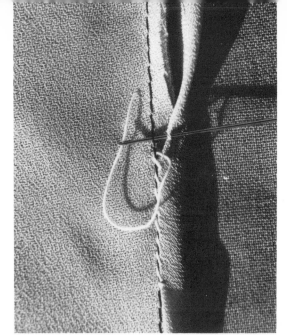

Double binding. In place of a facing, a bias strip may be folded in half and stitched to the edge

Above right The binding is turned over and the fold hemmed to the stitching line

Right Sheer fabrics can be neatened with a row of machining 5 mm from the seam line through both layers of fabric, followed by a row of zigzag machining if the material frays. The edge is trimmed to the machining

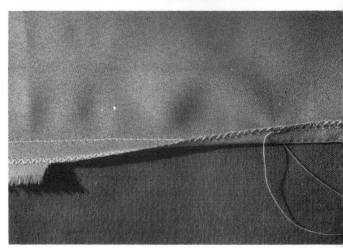

a flannelette sheet folded double and pinned firmly over the cutting-out board, or table, help to prevent the fabric slipping. If the selvage is tightly woven it may need to be clipped to allow the fabric to lie flat.

If the feed dog pulls at the fabric it will have to be stitched with tissue paper strips between the fabric and the machine. Sheer fabrics cannot be interfaced and facings too can spoil the effect. Self lining, or a sheer net, can be used and seams should be kept to a minimum. For the waistband where seams are necessary interfacing must be chosen to blend with the fabric, make the waistband firm, and disguise the seam allowances. Possibly a layer of interfacing and a layer of lining fabric will prove satisfactory.

The narrow machined hem, or rolled hem, are often used for sheers, although, where the fabric is underlined standard methods of putting up the hem are satisfactory. Lace which is not underlined may have a net facing applied about 6 cm wide. It should be folded in half and tacked to the right side of the garment, raw edges together. Two rows of machining close to the raw edge are made and the facing is then turned to the wrong side and slip stitched in place.

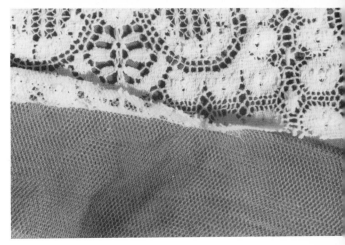

A hem for lace

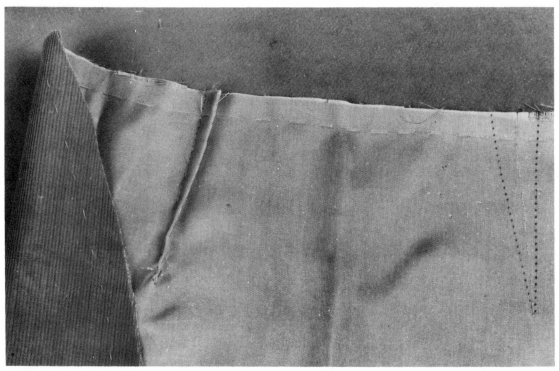

Interlining mounted on a skirt front with darts marked

Pile fabrics

Pile fabrics have a sleek, shiny, smooth surface, or a deep, rich one, depending on which direction the pile runs. The direction of the pile is judged by stroking the fabric. The direction of the pile should be marked on the wrong side with an arrow in tailor's chalk. The pile must run in the same direction on all pieces of the garment. If it runs from top to bottom the colour will be lighter and the appearance flat and shiny. Used this way the fabric wears well and sheds dust. With the pile running up, a deeper richer colour emerges and the pile looks thicker and richer. Formal and dress-wear are often made with the pile going up, and outer wear with it going down.

If the fabric slips while it is being cut it might prove easier to cut through a single thickness. This slipping may occur too during stitching which should be done in the direction of the pile. This is due to the action of the pile on the two layers of fabric pushing the seams out of line. A piece of tissue paper between the two layers prevents this and it can be torn away afterwards quite easily.

Simple styles and restrained details are best for pile fabrics. Creased edges should be avoided, getting fullness from unpressed pleats and flares.

Once velvet was a delicate fabric made of silk. Now it is often made from man-made fibres and may be crush, spot and water-resistant. It is a pile fabric and should be handled as a fabric with nap. There is a wide variety of velvet-like fabrics; velveteen, panne, crushed velvet, corduroy, and each one should be tested for the best method of stitching, neatening and pressing.

Lining

A lined skirt is usually much more comfortable to wear. Not only does it improve the appearance of the skirt, but very probably prolongs its life.

Lining fabrics are available in many different weights and colours. They may be woven or knitted. They must be chosen with the skirt fabric in mind, relating weights and fabric construction so that the lining does not overwhelm the skirt. They must be compatible too in the sense that if the skirt is washable, then the lining must be washable too. If the skirt fabric does not need ironing, then a non-iron lining must be found. If the lining is made from man-made fibres it should be anti-static so that it does not spoil the whole effect by clinging to the body beneath the skirt.

Basically there are two methods of lining:

Underlining involves mounting the pieces of the skirt on to the lining fabric before construction. Lining is cut and made up in a shape similar to the skirt, attached firmly at the waist and lightly to other seams.

Underlining

Underlining helps a skirt to keep its shape, improves crease resistance and provides a firm foundation. It also affects the hang of the skirt as the outer fabric takes on the weight of the underlining, giving a much more structured effect. Underlining is not suitable for gathered, or draped styles, unless it is used as a base, using a specially planned pattern piece on which the draped or gathered skirt is mounted.

Underlining pieces are usually cut from the same pattern pieces as the skirt, except that the hem allowance should be trimmed away from the underlining pieces. The pattern markings are put on the underlining fabric, not the actual skirt pieces. The lining and the outer fabric are then pinned and tacked together, matching notches. The two layers should also be tacked together along any fold lines, such as darts, tucks or pleats, to prevent any drifting movement during construction.

From this point the two fabrics are treated as one. The hem, when it is turned up and neatened, can be stitched to the underlining only, which gives a very smooth effect on the outside.

Lining

Skirt linings are also cut from the same pattern pieces as the skirt itself except that no waistband will be needed unless the fabric is sheer. The pattern markings will have to be transferred to both the outer skirt and the lining pieces as the two are constructed separately until the waistband stage is reached. The lining is made up in exactly the same way as the skirt: darts, seams, panels, except that it is made up with the right side of the material inside and all seams on the outside.

The lining should be attached to the skirt at the waist, wrong sides together, before the waistband is attached. The seam allowance on the lining is turned under where the skirt opening has been arranged and then slip-stitched to the back of the zip tape.

Where a gathered or pleated skirt is to be lined, the lining can be cut from an A-line pattern to keep bulk to a minimum and attached at the waistband in the usual way.

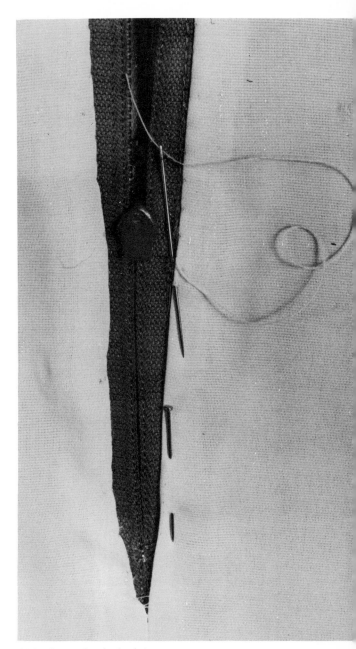

Lining hemmed to back of zip tape

Before cutting out the lining it must be decided whether it will be free hanging at the hem, or fixed to the hem of the skirt. A fixed lining is cut out the same length as the finished skirt, but the loose lining will need to be cut 2 cm longer than the finished hem to allow a 4 cm turning, making the finished lining 2 cm shorter than the finished length of the skirt. A loose lining will need a 2 cm

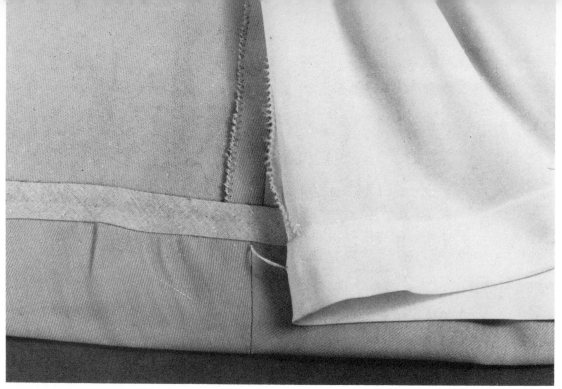

French tack 2 cm up from the bottom of the hem lining

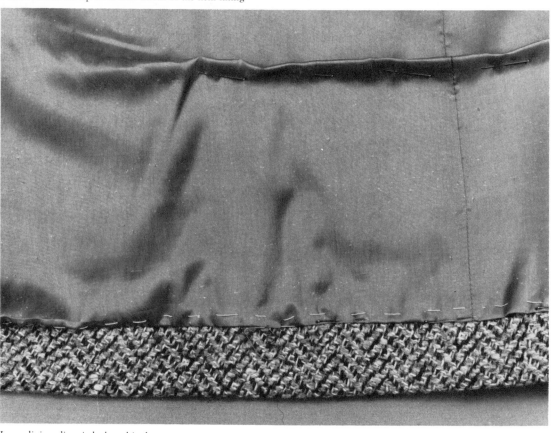

Loose lining slip stitched to skirt hem

french tack at the side seams, or panel seams about ɔ cm above the hem lining edge.

To attach a lining to a skirt at the hem

1 Turn up the skirt hem and attach it with blind stitches.

2 Pin a 1 cm tuck in the lining about 10 cm up from the bottom.

3 Make a 1 cm turning on the lining hem.

4 Slip stitch the hem of the lining to the hem of the skirt as it falls.

5 Take out the pinned tuck and press the lining down.

When the lining is fixed at the hem, the seam allowances need not be neatened unless the fabric is very loosely woven.

To prevent skirt linings from twisting they should be anchored with long, loose stitches at the seam allowances to the skirt. This is usually done at the side seams.

Decoration

Seams for decoration

The slot seam gives a tucked effect. A strip of fabric 4 cm wide is placed under the seam which may be similar to, or contrasting with, the main skirt fabric. It can be straight or bias cut. The seams to be joined are tacked together and the seam allowances pressed flat. The strip is laid along the wrong side of the seam allowance and tacked either side of the seam line. A row of machining is worked through all thicknesses at an even distance from each side of the seam line.

A piped seam has a folded bias strip which may have piping cord slotted in the fold, pinned and tacked to the right side of one section of the fabric with the fold extending beyond the seam line to the main part of the garment. The other section is put in position over it right sides together and the seam is then stitched in the normal way. Seam allowances are pressed to one side. For economy, if the seam is straight, straight pieces of fabric can be used for the piping strips.

Decorative stitching

Top-stitching is used to emphasise design details and structure lines and can be machined or hand sewn. The seam allowances are pressed open and if the material is not too thick it is pressed towards the side which is to be topstitched. Sometimes it is worked on either side of the stitched seam. To top-stitch by hand one or more rows of evenly spaced running stitches can be worked using buttonhole twist or embroidery floss. These stitches are usually at least 5 mm in length. This is known as glove stitch. Where a more strongly defined effect is wanted saddle stitch is used when longer stitches are made on the right side than on the wrong.

When the sewing machine is used it is necessary to experiment with contrasting threads, stitch lengths and widths, as well as machine tension. A size 16 needle and 6/8 stitches to 2.5 cm are reasonable starting points. Where a heavy thread is used it may have to be wound on to the bobbin and the top-stitching carried out wrong side up. Some machines have markings on the throat plate which can be used as a guide to even stitching but a

Slot seam

Strip of fabric placed behind tacked seam

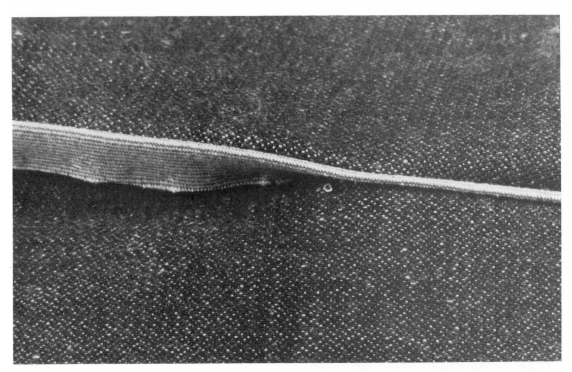

Piped seam

Right Top stitched pleats

strip of adhesive paper fixed at the appropriate distance from the needle will help. Where the stitching is not near an edge a quilting foot is useful but it may prove necessary to work to a tacked line.

Patch pockets are sometimes top-stitched before being slip stitched into position. Top-stitching on pleats holding them in place often as far as the hip is occasionally set back from the folded edge of the pleat and brought into the fold line, forming a tuck. Pleats are sometimes stitched close to the fold of the pleat for a crisper effect. Where the pleats are stitched down they should be top-stitched from the hem up to the point where they are to be held down. If the bobbin thread is cut the pleat can be laid over the skirt where it is to be stitched down and the machining continued without a break on the surface.

More elaborate effects can be achieved very simply by using embroidery stitches such as cross stitch, chain stitch and blanket stitch. The swing needle sewing machine makes it possible to produce a wide variety of repeat designs very quickly using various threads, stitch lengths and stitch widths.

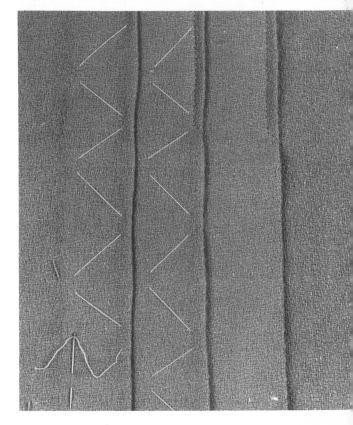

Two rows of running stitch threaded with a contrasting colour

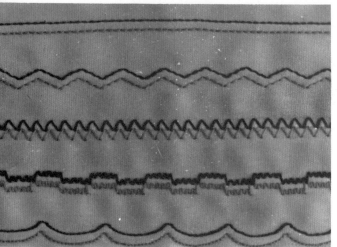

Machine embroidery

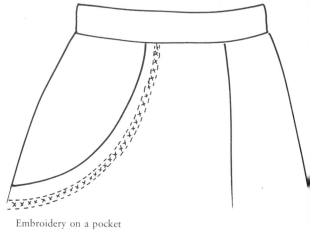

Embroidery on a pocket

An arrowhead tack can be embroidered at the end of a dart or at the bottom of a pleat. A triangle is marked which has three equal sides. The needle is brought up through the fabric at the lower left hand corner. A small stitch is taken at the top corner going from right to left. The needle is taken across the bottom of the triangle by going in through the bottom right hand corner and being brought out next to the stitch already made at the left hand corner. Work is continued down the sides and across the bottom, keeping the stitches close together until the entire triangle is covered by the thread. The crow's foot tack is also worked in a triangle but with indented sides. The needle is brought up through the fabric at any corner. Working clockwise a small stitch is taken at each corner in turn. The stitches are continued round the triangle each one worked close to the previous stitch until it is completely filled in.

Appliqué

Appliqué embroidery is very suitable for decoration on clothes as it is bold and quite quick to do. Simple shapes cut out in contrasting fabrics and colours can be attached in several different ways.

Fabrics which are very slippery or have a strong tendency to fray are best avoided although they can be backed with iron-on interfacing which would make them easier to handle. If zigzag machining is used to attach the pieces, then they are best cut bigger than the finished shape and trimmed close to the stitching after they have been attached. Blanket stitch and hemming stitch are suitable for attaching appliqué pieces. If fusible webbing is used, the piece can be ironed-on avoiding the need for sewing, although embroidery stitches might be used to highlight the design.

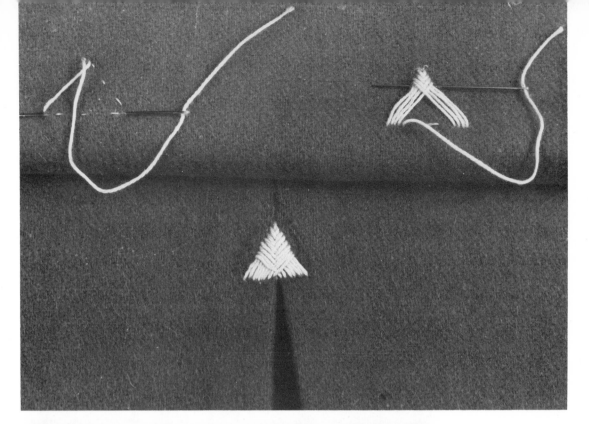

Arrowhead tack

Appliqué embroidery

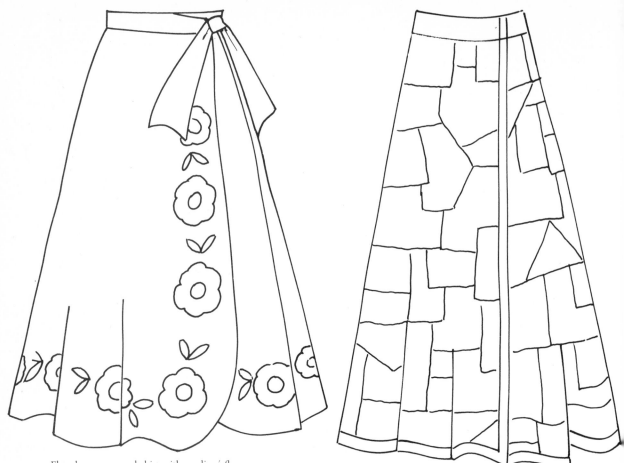

Flared wrap-around skirt with appliqué flowers

Patchwork

Random patchwork in which pieces are sewn together without planning is an easy way to make an individual skirt. The pieces can be joined together in the normal way, keeping the grain of each piece in line with the pieces already joined. If the skirt is lined there is of course no need to finish the raw edges. If the pieces are an awkward shape it might prove easier to press down the seam allowances and zigzag the pieces together from the right side.

Motifs of geometrical shapes may be used to decorate patch pockets or hems of skirts. The shape must be made in cardboard from which the required number of shapes is cut in paper. The fabric is tacked temporarily to the paper and the pieces hemmed together.

Quilting

Wadded or English quilting is sometimes used for decoration on pockets and hems, although sometimes the whole skirt is quilted. If the whole skirt is being quilted the fabric should be quilted before the pieces are cut out. The quilting may be in the form of traditional shapes, geometric shapes, outlining patchwork shapes or outlining the design printed on the fabric. It can be done by machine or by hand with small running stitches. The layers of material should be tacked together, backing, interlining or wadding and top layer and the quilting worked through these layers. If a small section of the skirt is being quilted, such as the hem, it should be worked after the pieces are cut out, allowing additional material all round so that after the quilting has been worked the piece can be re-cut to allow for the material which has been taken up in the quilting.

Italian or cord quilting gives a raised line effect. A channel is made by stitching through the outer fabric and a backing fabric and piping cord is threaded through the channel.

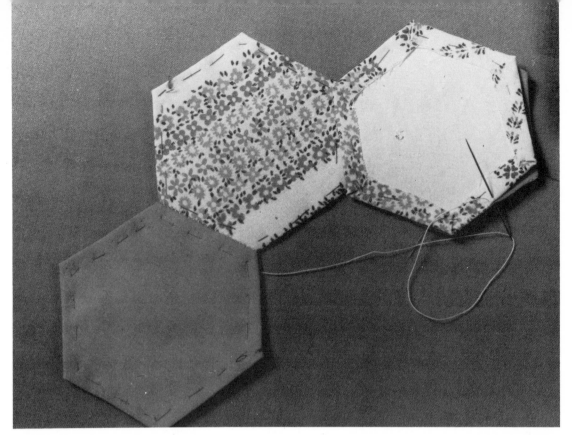

Patchwork-hexagon shapes being joined

Wadded or English quilting

Italian quilting at hem and waistband

Ribbon and ricrac braid trim

Italian quilting

Braids and lace

Several rows of braid can be sewn together, on top of one another, ricrac over ribbon, embroidery over ricrac. It can be plaited or twisted together before it is attached. It can outline a pocket, decorate a waistband or trim round the skirt anywhere between the waist and the hem. Before it is sewn on it should be pressed with a damp cloth to pre-shrink it and it should not be stretched as it is applied. Careful marking at the pattern stage with lines transferred by tracing wheel or tailors' tacks makes the application of flat braid by hand or machine very easy and quick. It is usually stitched on after the skirt is finished by either slip stitching or machining. If the braid can be joined neatly it can be attached to the skirt where it will be least noticed. If it frays it is better to open a construction seam just wider than the braid, slip the ends through and re-machine the seam. Soutache or narrow bias braid is very flexible and so is often used for designs incorporating curving lines. The design can be marked with tacking stitches and the soutache pinned over, easing it round corners. It is possible to machine it using a zipper foot but it is often applied by hand using matching thread and small running stitches through the centre of the braid.

Pre-folded braid is sometimes used as a piping decoration or it can be used to finish a hem, round pockets or on the waistband. It can be sewn on by hand or by machine. The braids are usually folded off centre so that they can be sewn on with the stitching concealed. The narrower of the two folded edges will be on the wrong side and can be sewn by hand or machine. On the right side the slightly wider layer can be stitched down and will cover the first row of stitching completely.

Ricrac braid is very versatile. It can be machined on with straight machining or machine embroidery can be worked over it to give a braid-like effect. It can be sewn on with embroidery thread which might catch the points or with a cross or

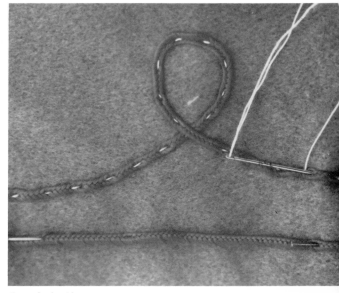

Soutache braid

Ricrac braid

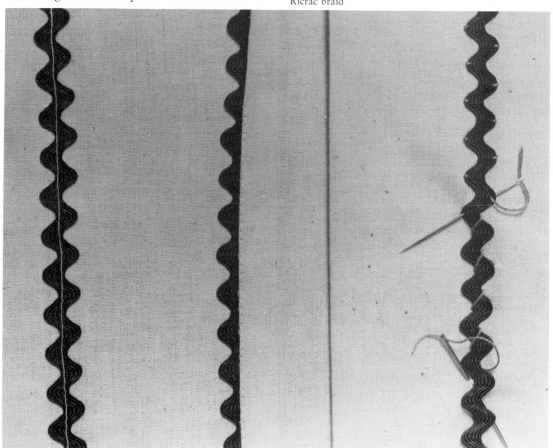

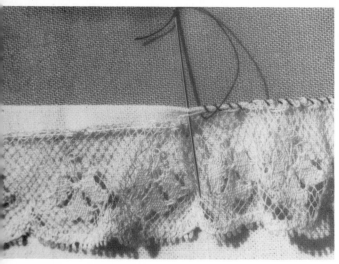

Whip stitching lace

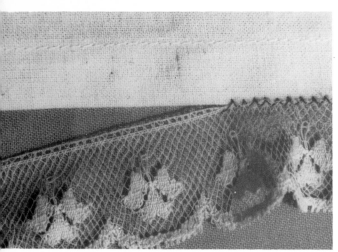

Attaching lace with zigzag machining

hem and the gathered edge of the lace. A quicker method is to lay the edge of the lace at the side of the fold of the hem and zigzag the two edges. Lace insertion has both edges finished in the same way and they may be either straight or scalloped. Lace insertion is tacked to the right side of the fabric and the edges of the lace are either sewn with a fine hemming stitch or zigzag machine stitch. The material is then cut away from behind the lace and trimmed close to the stitching. When joining lace bands they can either be seamed together with an open seam or overlapped and a small whipstitch worked round a motif. The underneath layer is then cut away.

Beads and sequins

Beads and sequins are added after the skirt is finished. The outline for the design to be worked is marked on the right side with chalk or tacking thread. The thread holding the beads must be drawn through beeswax to strengthen it. A beading needle is very long and thin to slide easily through the beads which are sewn on singly or several at a time with a back stitch. When several beads are strung along a thread the thread holding the beads is sewn to the skirt, taking a stitch between each bead. When sequins are sewn on singly they usually have a small bead in the centre which holds it in place. They are sometimes sewn on in rows with a back stitch. At the beginning of each stitch a sequin is threaded on to the needle and slid down until it lies flat when the thread is drawn up tight. Sequins and diamanté can be bought in strips as well as in the form of encrusted braids. These should be whip stitched by hand to the fabric, avoiding the sequin or diamanté. Beads, metal shapes and diamanté are available with metal clamps which are pushed through the fabric and straightened out on the back.

Belts

Thick waists probably look best with narrow belts of matching or darker fabric whereas the trim waisted can choose from a wider range. Belt-making kits are available and these are usually complete with buckles which can be covered according to individual taste with matching or contrasting fabrics.

All self belts should be stiffened so that they will retain their shape although tie belts need only a light interfacing. Straight belts can be stiffened with commercially produced belting, a heavy

half-cross stitch. It can be machined into a tuck or a seam so that only the points can be seen.

Flat braids come in various widths and may be sewn on in rows close together or far apart, side by side or covering or crossing each other. They can also be used for binding.

Lace can be used to make a skirt or can be used as an edging or an insertion. When it is used as an edging it may be gathered by drawing up the heavy thread in the upper edge before it is attached. After the edge has been drawn up sufficiently the ends of the thread are wound round a pin placed at right angles to the edge. The gathers should be adjusted so that they are even. Lace edging can be sewn on with a close whip stitch worked on the edge of the

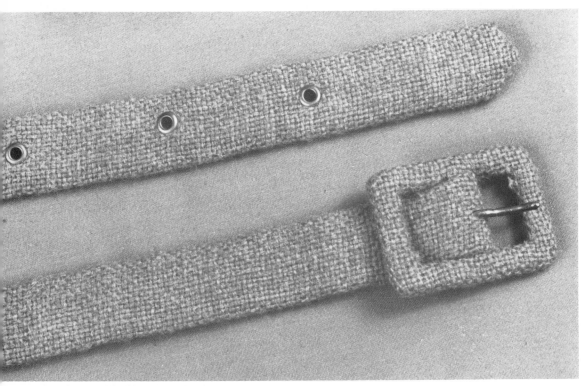

Belt with covered buckle and metal eyelets

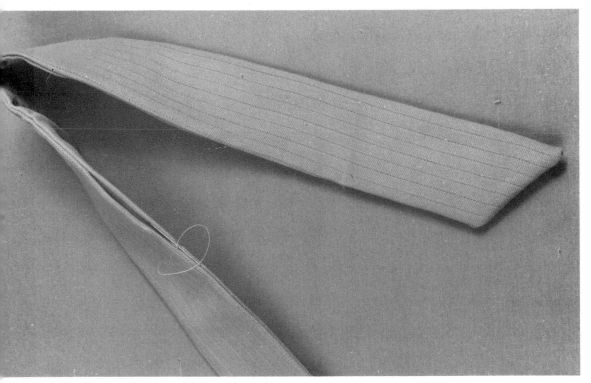

Tie belt with opening for turning left on one long side

Belt of plaited rouleau strips

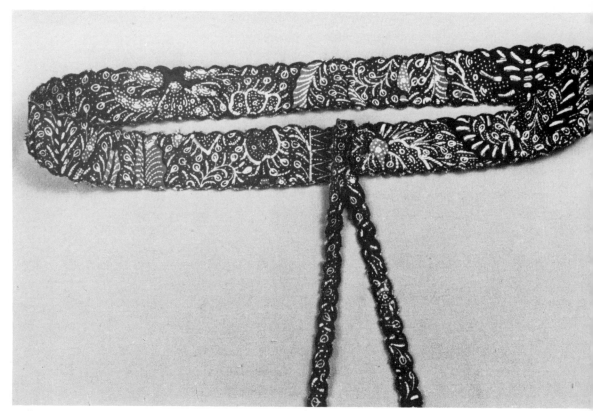

Stiffened belt with tie fastening. Shell edged by machine and trimmed close to the stitching

interfacing or canvas. They can be backed with self fabric or if this is bulky, grosgrain ribbon can be used which should be pre-shrunk. Belts which are buckled should be at least 15 cm longer than the waist measurement, including seam allowances. Buckles can be bought in a variety of colours and shapes as well as those designed to be covered with fabric. They should be about 3 mm wider than the finished width of the belt, measured on the inside.

A belt with interfacing is quite easy to make. The interfacing is either ironed or hemmed to the wrong side of the fabric. It can then be stitched round leaving an opening along one of the long sides for turning. This opening is slip stitched after the belt is turned right side out. A belt with interfacing can be top-stitched. When a belt is backed with grosgrain ribbon the fabric is tacked over the belt stiffening and the grosgrain ribbon slip stitched along the back. Fabric for a tie belt should be lightly interfaced and the lightweight iron-on is ideal. After the belt has been cut out the required length, and twice the finished depth plus seam allowance, it should be machined round all sides, leaving an opening of about 8 cm on one long side for turning. This opening should be slip stitched together when the belt has been turned.

Belts can be made with plaited lengths of rouleau, strips of macramé, braid, or crochet. They can be embroidered and decorated with appliqué or beads. Soft leather is machined quite easily although a triangular needle might be necessary for thicker leather.

A buckle with a prong needs an oblong opening at the straight end of the belt. Two holes are made with a stiletto about 6 mm apart and a slit cut between them. The opening should be finished with buttonhole stitch. Eyelets will be needed too. These are impossible to work through stiff commercial belting and metal eyelets in various colours can be bought which are fixed to the belt with a special tool. In softer fabrics a hole can be pierced with a stiletto and buttonhole stitched.

Pocket in a seam stitched round on the outside

Pockets

Pockets are useful and decorative. They are sometimes fitted into a seam, or attached to the surface when they are called patch pockets or they may be made through a slit especially made in the skirt.

When a pocket in a seam is put in a skirt of heavyweight fabric it is often made partly or completely of lining to reduce bulk. The side seam should be stitched leaving an opening for the pocket which can be tacked up and the whole seam pressed open. The pockets are stitched separately to the seam allowance of the skirt 1 cm from the edge. If the garment seam is to be pressed open the seam allowance must be clipped at the top and bottom of the pocket to the stitching line and both sections pressed towards the front. The outer edges of the pocket are machined together and the tacking removed from the opening.

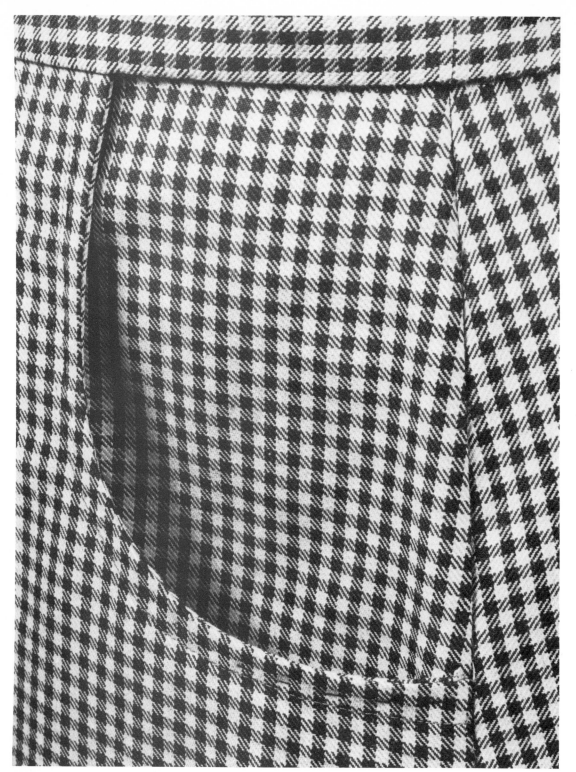

Hip pocket

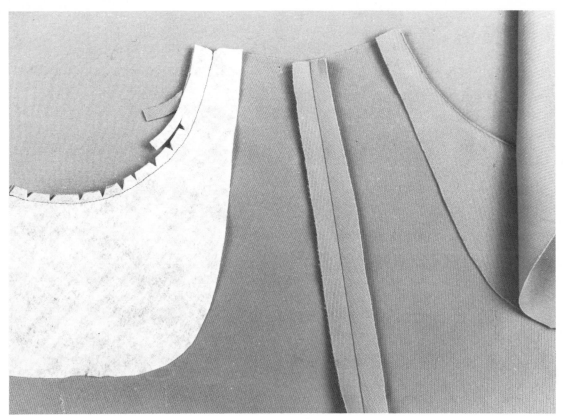

Hip pocket with interfacing attached

The pocket on the front hip is constructed before the side seams of the skirt are joined. The skirt should be interfaced at the front using the same pattern piece as for the inner pocket. The interfacing prevents the curved edge from stretching and supports the pocket. The interfacing is tacked to the wrong side of the skirt front and the inner pocket stitched to the right side of the skirt front. After clipping and grading, the inner pocket is turned to the inside, pressed and either top-stitched or under-stitched. The pocket section is stitched to the inner pocket round the edges and tacked to the side seams of the skirt and the waistline according to the design.

Patch pockets may be lined or unlined. For an unlined pocket the upper edge should be neatened and turned down on the right side along the fold-line marking. The pocket should be stitched round along the seam line and the seam allowance trimmed to about 6 cm and trimmed according to its shape. The top hem allowance is turned to the wrong side and pressed. The seam allowances are turned under along the line of stitching and

tacked. The pocket can be machined into place on the skirt with a small triangle or double row of stitches to reinforce it at the corners, where it may get heavy wear. It can be machined just to the corners and the ends fastened off or it can be slip stitched in place with very fine stitches. A very neat finish is given if it is attached from the back with close back stitches. When a pocket is lined the lining must be slightly smaller than the pocket so that the lining does not show on the right side. The lining can be machined to the pocket by attaching the lining to the right side of the pocket at the upper edge, leaving an opening at the centre of the seam. The pocket is folded at the seam line right sides together and machined round the outer edges. After trimming, the pocket is turned right sides out through the opening which is then slip stitched. When the lining is attached by hand it is easier to make sure that the lining is brought to the inside of the pocket and will not show if the pocket is top-stitched on. The lining is joined to the pocket right sides together along the top. The seam allowances are turned in all round and then

Unlined patch pocket

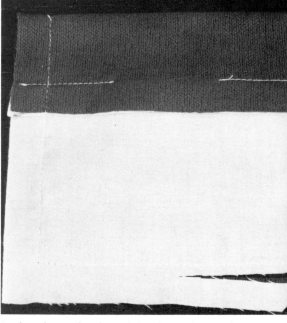

Patch pocket machined round the edges and trimmed

Left Lining joined to the pocket with opening for turning

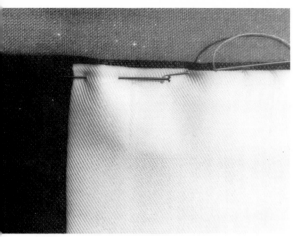

Lining hemmed to pocket

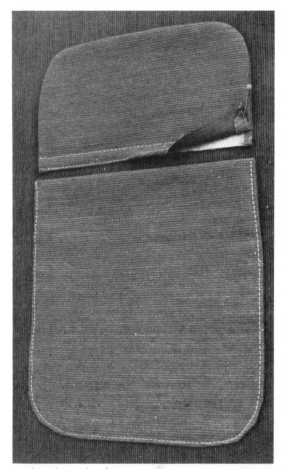

Patch pocket with a flap

the pocket is folded over. The lining is slip stitched in place round the edges. Sometimes a patch pocket has a flap and this needs to be interfaced. The flap is machined in place above the pocket. The seam allowance nearest to the skirt is trimmed to 4 mm and the one above it folded over and machined or slip stitched.

The easiest pocket in a slit is the one-piece bound pocket which is very similar in construction to the bound buttonhole using the patch method. The pocket fabric should be cut 2.5 cm wider than the opening and twice the depth of the finished pocket plus 2.5 cm allowance for the binding. The pocket bag is creased 2.5 cm below the centre and then placed on the skirt right sides together with the

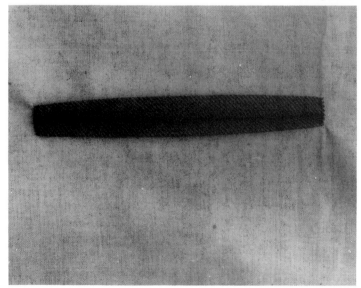

Bound pocket

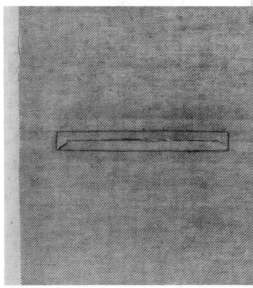

Pocket bag machined on wrong side

crease against the marked pocket and the shorter piece below the opening. On the wrong side the pocket is machined 6 mm from each side of the opening and across the ends. A cut is made through the centre of the marking and diagonally into the corners to the corner of the stitching. The pocket is pulled through the slit to the wrong side and the folded edges brought together to form an even binding on each side of the opening on the right side. An inverted pleat will form at each end of the pocket opening on the wrong side. On the right side the pocket is stitched round the seam line between the binding and the skirt. The upper section of the pocket is folded down and stitched to the lower section round the edges.

A welt pocket consists of a flap or welt which is interfaced and may be backed with lining. It has two pocket sections usually made of lining which are cut the depth of the finished pocket plus seam allowances and the width of the finished pocket again plus seam allowances. If the welt pocket is not horizontal, the shape of the pocket bag must be adjusted so that it will hang down. The welt is tacked to the right side of the skirt with the edge of the flap to the line marking the pocket position. One pocket section is tacked over this. Working on the wrong side the pocket is machined round

Pocket pushed through to wrong side of skirt

Binding stitched round seam line

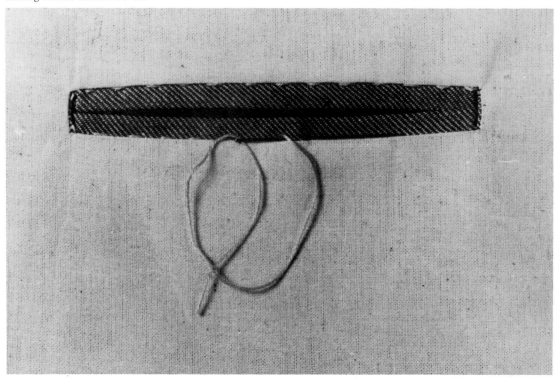

the marked opening and the opening cut. The pocket is pushed through the slit to the wrong side and the opening tacked round the edge. The back of the pocket is stitched to the section already attached, round the edges. The edges of the welt are top-stitched or slip stitched to the skirt.

The flap pocket has a flap section which is left loose at the sides and two pocket sections which are made either entirely of the fabric of the skirt or the upper 6 cm or so which might show when the flap is lifted is made of self fabric and the remainder of lining. The flap is tacked to the right side, raw edges to the pocket position with one inner section tacked over the top. On the wrong side the pocket is machined round the opening and across the ends with the lower edge slightly shorter so that the corners will not show when the flap is pressed down. The pocket piece is drawn through to the wrong side and a section of the pocket is folded up to form a tuck at the bottom edge, wide enough to fill the gap. This is stitched in position close to the seam line at the lower edge of the opening. On the inside the ends of the tuck are stitched, catching the small triangles which formed at the ends of the pocket opening when it was cut diagonally at the corners. The remaining pocket piece is stitched in place round the edges.

Welt and one pocket section machined in place and slit

Stitching line for flap pocket. Corners may be strengthened with interfacing

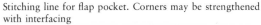

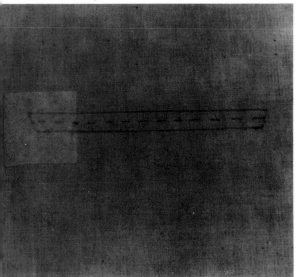

Welt laid on right side ready for stitching down

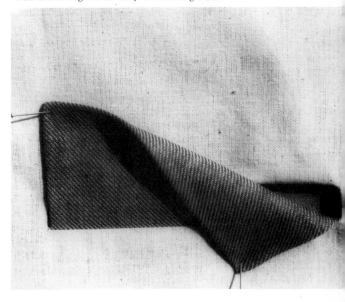

Tuck and triangle stitched

Remaining pocket piece in place

Frills

Frills are strips of fabric which are gathered or pleated at one edge and joined to another part of the skirt. Straight frills are cut on the lengthwise grain and are usually from $1\frac{1}{2}$ to 3 times the length of the edge to which they are to be attached. The wider the frill the more fullness will be needed. The lower edge of a frill can be hemmed but often a narrow double turning is machined.

The edge which is to be gathered should have two rows of machine stitches using the longest stitch close to the edge, about 4 and 7 mm away from the raw edge. For a long heavy frill, buttonhole twist which will not break when being drawn up may prove easier to use than regular thread for the gathering stitches. After drawing up the bobbin thread to make the gathers, the ends are wound round a pin to hold them until the frill is attached. Where there is a wide area to gather it is easier to divide both the frill and the skirt into sections, quarters at least, and pin these together drawing up the frill between the marking pins. The two rows of gathering should be started at the same place along the frill so that the ends are together. After the frill has been machined to the skirt the two edges of the frill and the skirt can be neatened as one piece of fabric by binding or zigzagging close to the seam line, the excess seam allowance being trimmed away.

Shirring may or may not be elasticated. It can be made up of several rows of gathering, perhaps as many as eight and it is usually worked on lightweight fabrics which are drawn up to the right measurement. The back needs to be re-inforced by a piece of self fabric cut to fit without the gathers and hemmed in place over the gathers to act as a support.

Elastic shirring is used at the top of pockets and at the waistline of skirts but it is only suitable for lightweight fabrics. Several rows are needed to provide enough elasticity for the skirt to grip the waist. The elastic thread should be wound on the bobbin by hand, stretching it very slightly and winding it firmly. The machine should be set on a long stitch, about 7 cm to 2.5 cm and the tension should be checked. Working on the right side, the fabric should be held straight as it is stitched. The fabric should be stretched flat as each row is worked and the ends of each row tied, later to be held in the seams.

Circular frills may give a similar effect to a gathered frill but the fullness is only at the outer

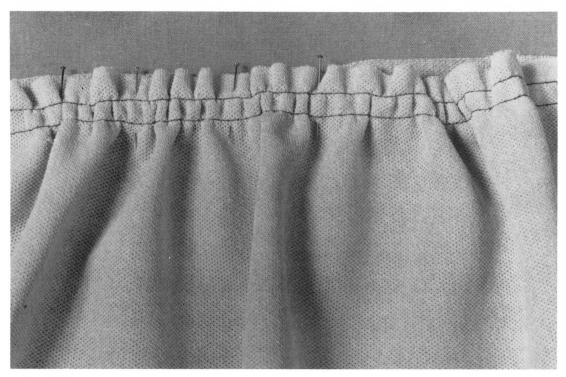

Gathered frill

Frill neatened with zigzag machining

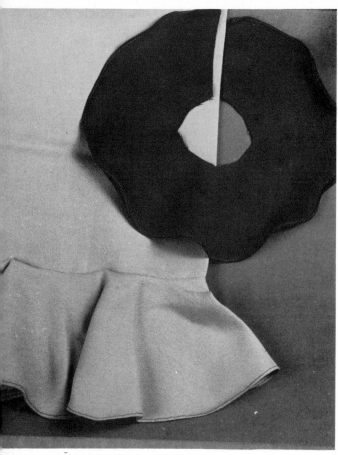

Circular frills

edge. The edge which is joined to the skirt fits
smoothly without fullness. This effect is obtained
by cutting ruffles with curved edges. The inner
edge is much smaller than the outer. On very thin
materials frills cut from curves and circles may be
lined by joining them along the outer edges right
sides together and turning them right sides out
before they are attached, but on heavier materials a
narrow machined hem is more usual.

Index